A GUIDE TO PLANNING THE ULTIMATE FOOTPATH...

the *LAND'S END TO JOHN O'GROATS walk*

...WALKING ADVENTURE BY ANDREW MCCLOY

The Land's End to John o'Groats Walk *1st edition 2002.*

Published by Cordee, *3a DeMontfort Street, Leicester LE1 7HD. www.cordee.co.uk*

Copyright *© Andrew McCloy 2002.*

ISBN 1 871890 59 4

Photography by Andrew McCloy, Jerry Rawson and Gordon Gadsby. Cover Trail Magazine

Design Mike Dunmore. Repro Prestige Filmsetters, Leicester.
Printed by Fratelli Spada SpA, Rome.

CONTENTS

Land's End

INTRODUCTION

PLANNING &
PRACTICAL CONSIDERATIONS

There's a special magic about the phrase 'Land's End to John o'Groats'. The names conjure up romantic images of challenge and adventure, and the ultimate journey to the opposite ends of the kingdom! At Land's End you're on the fingertip of the South West peninsula looking out into the vastness of the Atlantic; while at the northern extremity the cold seas stretch out towards Scandinavia and the Arctic Circle. Distance-wise, Land's End and John o'Groats represent the two points furthest apart on the British mainland, but if you want to be pedantic Dunnet Head and not John o'Groats is the most northerly tip; and of course southwards it's Lizard Point.

Britain's small, island setting makes an 'End to End' notion both complete and obtainable. The range of scenery on offer, the relatively good climate, the level of public access and proliferation and variety of paths and trails - this and the fact that the average LEJOG walk of around 1,000-1,200 miles/1,609-1,930km is within the capabilities of most fit adults makes the End to End Walk a highly attractive proposition. And in addition to the distance, there is the added challenge of determining your route. The roadwalkers can leave Cornwall on the A30 and enter Caithness on the A9 without treading a footpath in between. Fine if you like the constant sound and smell of traffic, or doing something wacky like pushing a pram, or sticking close to motorised back-up all the way. On the other hand the whole essence of the End to End Walk for a large number of people is that walking from one end of Britain to the other is entirely possible without resource to main roads. You can walk cliff paths, old railway tracks, packhorse routes, canal towpaths, field paths, bridleways, National Trails, country parks, green lanes, open moorland, river banks, and so on, and have the most extraordinarily varied and rewarding walk possible. Sure, there are some sections, notably in northern Scotland, where surfaced lanes probably provide the most practical route, but the vast majority of the walk can easily be achieved well away from busy roads.

So what's the best LEJOG walking route? Ten years ago, researching my first End to End guide, I came up with three possibilities. An energetic West Coast passage was provided by the South West Coast Path and the Offa's Dyke Path, the fells of the Lake District and the Southern Uplands, but in between there were too many dull or lowland urban sections. Likewise my East Coast route had its highlights (the Ridgeway and The Fens, Lincolnshire Wolds and the Cleveland Way cliffs) but its indulgent and wandering course cost too many miles. The most popular choice for discerning End to End walkers turned out to be a central route that fringed Dartmoor and traversed the Somerset Levels and Mendips, strode along the top of the Cotswolds and Pennines, and sampled the thrills of the West Highlands of Scotland, while all the time keeping its sights on that far-off north-eastern tip. However, since the mid 1990s new trails have been completed (Severn Way, St Cuthbert's Way) and others begun (Great Glen Way, Land's End Trail, Pennine Bridleway), so it's now time for an up-to-date look at the ultimate Land's End to John o'Groats Walk in terms of both quality of scenery and overall directness. But as before I've suggested a number of alternative route sections, involving such majestic trails as the South West Coast Path and Offa's Dyke Path, plus a route through the Cairngorms.

It's important to point out that this book is intended to provide an overview, a framework if you like, for the big walk. To properly and safely walk the whole distance on the ground you'll need to scrutinise the component guidebooks and/or maps listed, especially for the more remote and wilder locations further north. Also take heed of the notes on preparation and equipment, however much experience you already have under your belt. The following pages provide a summary of everything you need to know for getting from one end of Great to Britain to the other on foot. All you have to do is to go out and walk it.

THE LAND'S END TO JOHN O'GROATS WALK: A SHORT HISTORY

The earliest records of walks that deliberately linked the two ends of Britain date from the 1840s, but are inevitably sketchy. In 1863 an American called Elihu Burritt walked from London to John o'Groats, then afterwards from London to Land's End; and in 1871 two brothers, John and Paul Naylor, set out to walk from John o'Groats to Land's End on a wandering route (they carried no maps) in which they abstained from intoxicating drink and tobacco and attended two religious services every Sunday.

Despite sporadic completions in the next 90 years popular interest in the End to End idea didn't really take off until 1960, when Dr Barbara Moore completed the journey in an extraordinary walk taking just 22 days. Born in Russia as Anya Cherkasova, she was imprisoned during the Russian Revolution, then emerged to become the USSR's first woman aviator and a motoring and motor-cycling champion before moving to India and taking up meditation. Eccentric in just about every way possible, she had previously walked from Edinburgh to London with her blistered feet tied only in sacking - in a deliberate echo of the Russian peasantry of her youth. Her three-week End to End walk generated huge media interest, and was all the more notable given her strict vegetarian diet of fruit juice, honey and green vegetables and the fact that she had to battle her way through some appalling weather conditions. Dr Moore, who went on to walk from San Francisco to New York in 85 days, died in 1977 at the age of 73.

Like any good entrepreneur, holiday camp supremo Billy Butlin was quick to jump on the bandwagon and within a few months of Barbara Moore's walk he announced that he was organising a challenge walk from Land's End to John o'Groats with prize money of over £5,000. Entrance was open to all-comers, but this was a time when recreational long distance walking was distinctly uncommon - the opening of Britain's first official trail, the Pennine Way, was still five years away. So looking back on the event now it was no surprise that some of those setting off from north east Scotland were hopelessly ill-prepared, dressed in unsuitable clothes and with next to no experience of walking long distances. But there again Billy Butlin and the race organisers had no idea either: they gave the entrants barely a fortnight to prepare, and began the race at John o'Groats at the end of February. Those selected to take part were sent an official letter of acceptance, with the following advice: "As you get along the road, of course, you will find things a little easier but many of the wise ones will use the night-time for travelling and get their rest periods during daylight when facilities are bound to be more readily available."

Amid enormous publicity the race went ahead as planned, despite treacherously cold and icy conditions, and after the inevitable retirements (and disqualifications for cheating) only 138 out of the 715 that set off finally made it to Land's End. The first to arrive was Jim Musgrave, who took just 15 days, 14 hours and 31 minutes; and the first woman was Wendy Lewis, a young apprentice hairdresser from Liverpool, who arrived two days later. Lewis, who died in 1999 aged 55, had actually set out on her own End to End walk (with her sister Joy) before Butlin's race was announced - and then promptly returned to Scotland to do it all again. The excitement, hardship and naivety surrounding the competition is described from the point of view of an entrant in a fascinating book, The Big Walk, by someone calling themselves 'A. Walker'.

Since the 1960s the Land's End to John o'Groats journey has established itself in the national conscience, and above all else in the record books. The challenge of joining End to End seems to offer that obsessive fascination that is held by Munro-bagging and the Three Peaks Challenge (linking Snowdon, Scafell Pike and Ben Nevis in the shortest possible time). But, like the Three Peaks Challenge, the quickest and most direct route is inevitably by road, and of course it gradually gets quicker over time as new by-passes and bridges are built. For what it's worth, the LEJOG walking record is held by Malcolm Barnish of the 19th Regiment, Royal Artillery, who in June 1986 took just 12 days, 3 hours and 45 minutes to walk from End to End; and the women's record is held by Ann Sayer, with a time of 13 days, 17 hours and 42 minutes, in October 1980. According to most experts the shortest possible LEJOG walking route - exclusively roadside, of course - is currently 868 miles/1,397km,

although the famous signpost at Land's End states John o'Groats is
874 miles/1,406km distant. But do you really want to walk alongside
traffic all that way?

And then there are the nutters. In May 1990 Arvind Pandya from India
took 26 days and 7 hours to join one end of Britain to the other - by
running backwards (he has also run backwards across the USA). Steve
Fagan took nine days to roller skate from End to End; someone was
literally posted to John o'Groats as first class mail; and two brothers-in-
law spent 30 days of their lives taking turns to push each other in a
wheelbarrow the entire distance. Well done, guys - time well spent.
It seems the most favoured method of propulsion is by bicycle, although
few come close to matching the record set in 1990 by Andy Wilkinson
who cycled from Land's End to John o'Groats in just 1 day, 21 hours,
2 minutes and 19 seconds! And for the record a McDonnell F-4K
Phantom jet did it in 46 minutes and 44 seconds in 1988.

Ever since The Big Walk the library of published End to End accounts
has continued to grow, and encompasses everything from well-written
outdoor classics through to cheerful if distinctly amateur diaries.
However, there are two books that are rooted firmly in the former camp,
and although a little dated are still recommended reading for aspiring End
to Enders who choose the footpath over the highway. Journey Through
Britain by John Hillaby was published in 1968 and remains the first and
arguably the best account of a modern End to End walk, and his thoughts
on walking and the lot of the long-distance solo walker will strike a chord.
And if you, too, are planning a foray through the North West Highlands
of Scotland check out his account of traversing Ben Mor Assynt in the
mist. Meanwhile Hamish's Groats End Walk (1981) is a thoughtful
and enjoyable tale of a five month walk of 2,500 miles/4,022km by
Hamish Brown and his dog that began at John o'Groats and took in the
highest peaks of Scotland, England, Wales and Ireland (he sailed from
Anglesey and then walked all the way across southern Ireland). The most
imaginative End to End return journey was undertaken in 1978 by John
Merrill who completed the first, continuous walk around the British
coastline (England, Scotland and Wales). The total mileage came to 6,824
miles/10,980km, and his published diary-like account, Turn Right at
Land's End, gives a good flavour of what it was like to average 26
miles/42km a day and deal with the unrelenting public and media
pressure.In addition to these three books, the growing library of published
End to End accounts includes heroic tales of battles with blisters, bossy
B&B landladies and Pennine bogs; and there's even a self-styled
'grandparents' guide' for walking from Land's End to John o'Groats! A
selection of these titles are listed in Chapter 7. It all goes to prove that the
End to End Walk remains, quite simply, an adventure of a lifetime.

JOHN O'GROATS

BRORA

INVERNESS

FORT WILLIAM

ROWARDENNAN

EDINBURGH

JEDBURGH

DUFTON

MALHAM

EDALE

PENKRIDGE

TEWKESBURY

BATH

TIVERTON

ST BREWARD

LAND'S END

WHICH WAY ROUND?

There is no accepted or correct direction of walking. On balance probably more people begin at Land's End and head north, since Cornwall's southerly position usually ensures more benign weather conditions earlier on, and of course leaves the tougher hills and mountains for the weeks to come when hopefully you will be stronger and fitter (although the North Cornwall and Devon coast path is exacting enough if you choose that route). Incidentally, most End to End cyclists choose to start at Land's End due to the prevailing winds (generally at your back, not against you) which are said to save at least two days on the northbound journey. But of course it's all down to personal preference, and obvious factors such as where you live, what time of year you set off, and whether you want to toast your success with a few days in the Orkneys or a weekend on a sunny beach in the Scillies or South Devon. To help you choose, here's a rather subjective list of pros and cons:

STARTING AT LAND'S END
For:
Generally mild climate.
Easy to reach by public transport.
Gentle terrain in first few weeks (depending on route).
Plenty of amenities (B&Bs, pubs, shops, etc).
Allows earlier start in year (northern hills left for improving weather/daylight).
Against:
Overcrowded in peak season.
Tough coast path (depending on route).
Sense of heading 'uphill' to Scotland!
Danger of running into the Scottish midge season (Jul/Aug).
Walking through Cornwall and Devon seems to take forever.

STARTING AT JOHN O'GROATS
For:
Quiet location.
Gets the mountains out of the way early.
Quickly improves your fitness and stamina.
Less overall traffic and tourist fuss.
Psychologically 'downhill' to southern England!
Against:
Lack of amenities.
Difficult to reach.
Some roadwalking inevitable in first few days.
High and remote terrain early on.
Potential of cold/wet weather.

GETTING THERE

Penzance is served by trains and express coaches from London and other points around England, and from there local buses or taxis will take you the short distance to Land's End itself. Trains also run to Wick and Thurso in the far north of Scotland (change at Inverness), and from both these locations there are buses or taxis to John o'Groats. However, it is always a good idea to check with the relevant tourist information centre as timetables can change and services are not always frequent.

AN END TO END WALKING ROUTE

So, down to the nitty gritty. You've decided that you're going to walk from Land's End to John o'Groats (or vice versa) off-road as much as possible, following where appropriate or feasible existing long distance footpaths. Some of these, like the Pennine Way, will lead you for hundreds of miles, while others may transport you for little more than a day. The trails will not necessarily follow the most direct course, but unless you want to suffer main roads and urban centres it's by and large wise to persevere with them; and you can rest assured that the ever-changing scenery will be worth it. You'll also come to realise that major trails such as the West Highland Way encourage a useful support 'industry' such as cafes, bunkhouses, and so on; and the YHA will even book all your hostel beds in advance for you along the whole of the Pennine Way.

However, as far as the overall route is concerned a glance at the map will show that despite Britain's developing trail system there are a few clear and inevitable kinks in the main End to End course.
In its 1,150miles/1,850km the route faces a number of obstacles and has to make certain choices, so that along the way you will find some suggested 'Alternative Routes' to whet your appetite and stimulate ideas.
For instance, the rigorous South West Coast Path provides the first alternative to the main route, as it follows wandering tracks and lanes of central Cornwall and Devon; while further on, the urban centres of the English Midlands provide a significant barrier, and hence the Offa's Dyke Path option (included in many people's End to End walking routes over the years). But this does tend to lead rather off-course the nearer it gets to the Irish Sea, which means you then have to cut back across to the Pennines as there are few pleasant walking routes through the industrial North West. Similarly, Glasgow and Edinburgh are the two large obstacles to the Scottish mountains that face the northbound walker, and at the moment there's no single trail or established linking route from the Southern Upland Way to the West Highland Way (although Glasgow's local trails such as the Clyde and Kelvin Walkways may offer long-term possibilities). Once beyond the Central Lowlands the main End to End

Exe Valley Way

route, in order to utilise Scotland's limited trail system and visit some
spectacular scenery, veers north-westwards to Fort William before
returning along the Great Glen. But the more obvious and direct route,
outlined as an Alternative Route but almost certainly some people's first
preference, is to head northwards into the heart of the Grampians.
The final problem sees the far north-eastern seaboard of Caithness, narrow
and pathless, force most End to Enders on to tarmac, so that an
Alternative Route inland is a possible solution.

Mention should also be made at this point of the emerging National Cycle
Network, which although chiefly designed for bicycles does have a spin-off
use for long-distance walkers on ambitious journeys such as the End to
End Walk. The cycle charity Sustrans, who are masterminding the
network's development, plan to create a 10,000-mile countrywide network
of safe cycle routes by 2005, and although many of the principal routes
will be along lanes and minor roads they will also involve converted railway
lines, new traffic-free routes, and so on, and in some instances this can
prove very useful. Already the End to End Walk shares some small sections
of its route with what are now defined parts of the National Cycle
Network, such as the Camel Trail in Devon, across the Somerset Levels
near Glastonbury, and around the hinterland of Edinburgh.

Where the End to End Walk occasionally uses the likes of country lanes,
canal towpaths and, of course, cycle trails, there is very little need for route
description. Similarly, well-trodden long distance walking trails are usually
quite easy to follow, since not only will there be other walkers or their
bootprints to follow but you'll also be assisted by waymarks and signposts,
plus guidebooks and maps. Waymarks for the official trails are fairly
standard (acorns for National Trails in England and Wales, and usually a
thistle for their counterparts in Scotland), but for other trails they are
pleasantly varied in both design and spread - so don't expect a sign at every
turn. Guidebooks also vary in their make-up and usefulness, and although
most contain detailed maps and handy background information they do of
course become dated fairly quickly; and don't forget that just a handful of
books will add considerably to the weight of your pack. But the ultimate
(and in many ways still the best) route guide are Ordnance Survey maps,
and the good news for the aspiring End to Ender is that thanks to the new
Explorer series they are getting better and better. At a scale of 1:25 000
the orange-covered Explorer maps show individual paths and tracks in
great detail, and better still they also depict the specific route of National
Trails and now also many local walking trails, or 'Recreational Paths' as
they call them (such as the Exe Valley Way, Severn Way, Staffordshire
Way and Limestone Way). This, of course, means you don't have to carry a
whole library of guidebooks, plus it gives you ample opportunity to plan
route deviations and check, measure and scrutinise your overall passage in

considerable detail. Inevitably, because of the more detailed scale you'll need to take a greater number (plus the relevant and complementary Outdoor Leisure titles) than if you just stuck to the 1:50 000 Landranger series, but the Explorer series is newly-mapped and accurate, and its clear and detailed coverage is second to none. For a complete guide to the new Explorer range contact the Ordnance Survey for a copy of their free and indispensable Mapping Index (see Useful Addresses, Chapter 7).

PLANNING, PREPARATION AND EQUIPMENT

Any walk of over 1,000 miles is a major undertaking, whether or not you go by path or road, alone or with back-up. First of all you must consider some basic questions in terms of route and direction, time of year, alone or in company, continuous or in stages, tent or B&Bs/youth hostels (or both), time or money constraints, daily distances, and so on. The 1,147 miles/1,845km of the main End to End route as outlined in this book is broken down into 69 day stages (just under ten weeks), averaging out at 16.6 miles/26.7km a day. This, it goes without saying, is just a suggested timetable. There are a number of stages that could be strung together to shorten the overall time, just as there's ample opportunity to reduce the daily mileage and take far longer.

There are no hard and fast rules. A middle aged couple I once spoke to had been walking from Land's End to John o'Groats in regular fortnightly stages, twice a year, picking up their route where they had left off previously. It was a still a genuine walk from one end of the country to the other, but it fitted in much better in terms of overall affordability, work commitments, and so on. The only drawback to this approach is that membership of the End to End Club is only open to those completing continuous End to End journeys (they supply you with a verification form which you have to get stamped at either end, as well as at a selection of post offices in between).

Your timetable can be far more flexible if you carry camping equipment, and indeed many End to Enders opt for the self-sufficiency of a tent while allowing themselves the luxury of an occasional roof over their head in order to dry out, do some washing, take a bath, etc. If you rely solely on B&Bs and hostels you'll have to plan your timetable carefully, and in popular places (and at times like weekends and bank holidays) it is a good idea to book in advance. Local tourist information centres (TIC's) are always a mine of information in terms of B&Bs and campsites, as is The Rambler's Yearbook & Accommodation Guide; and also look out for dedicated accommodation lists to certain trails.

Daily mileage also depends on obvious points like walking speeds.

If there's four of you in a group your stage distances will inevitably be dictated by the slowest member's pace, so it's important not to be over-ambitious when planning your schedule. At the end of the day all will come to nought if you haven't prepared yourself physically and mentally. The latter is a case of thinking the whole project through or perhaps discussing it with friends or family, and considering all the potential problems or hazards and how you would react and cope. What would you do if you were benighted on the moors? Have you ever had to deal with a total drenching by heavy rain? Can you cope with your own company for long periods, or if you're walking in a small group do you know those people well enough to be able to get on in all situations? Sure, it's not like you're climbing the Eiger, but there again it's not a stroll to the cornershop either.

As far as physical preparation is concerned there's no excuses. If you simply get off the train at Penzance with a couple of weekends on the Cotswolds under your belt you're asking for trouble. If you haven't carried a full pack since your days as a Venture Scout then it's more than likely you're going to be in for a nasty surprise. With a walk of over 1,000 miles ahead of you, and a daily physical pounding over all manner of terrain, the ideal preparation is threefold. First, get yourself into shape over time through regular walking, swimming, cycling, jogging, or whatever. Second, strengthen your feet and legs by a regular programme of walking (you don't have to walk miles and miles every day, just do it regularly). And third, with The Walk approaching take your full pack and boots and go off and walk a medium-length long distance trail, such as the Wolds Way, Pembrokeshire Coast Path or the South Downs Way, and see how you get on. Over the years there have been plenty of people who have set out on the End to End Walk with minimal preparation, and many of them have simply never made it. And their stories never make good reading.

So what do you take with you? There's a fair degree of personal preference here: some people wear shorts in all weathers, walking poles have their champions, others prefer gaiters to overtrousers, and so on. A lot depends on the season you set off (woolly hat or peaked cap?), but camping gear aside, waterproofs must be packed at virtually any time of the year. A robust pair of walking boots, leather or fabric, is still probably the best choice for footwear, and of course offers the best grip and ankle protection over rough ground. But sports sandals have also become popular in recent years; and a tough pair of trainers are still as good as any on hard surfaces. Whatever you decide to wear on your feet the all-important point is to break your footwear in before you start the Walk - if you're purchasing a new pair of boots specifically for the End to End make sure that you get used to them well before you set off and so reduce the likelihood of sore

Tan Hill Inn, Pennine Way

feet and blisters. (Likewise, if you know your boots will give way before
the end of the Walk make sure that you have some replacements lined up
that are also properly walked-in.) The monthly walking magazines have
regular gear features and reviews which can be helpful, and there are plenty
of general guides to walking and backpacking which suggest all manner of
equipment checklists.

Among the important items of safety you will need to carry are a torch
and whistle, basic first aid kit and survival bag, plus of course a compass.
Things like binoculars, camera, diary, reading or identification book, etc,
will depend on what kind of weight you want on your back for ten weeks.
Maps have already been alluded to, and since you will need as many as
50 separate sheets they will likely or not end up taking quite a bit of room.
Unless you want to buy them all for posterity try and borrow them from
friends, public libraries, or the Ramblers' Association's Map Library.
As you progress along your walk post them home in batches (you can also
do this with socks, worn-out boots and so on!); and conversely you
can also pick up parcels of maps for the route ahead left with your auntie
in Uttoxeter that you haven't seen in six years, or poste restante at a
specific post office. This last is also a useful place at which to withdraw
money if you have something like a National Savings account (you can
always open one just for the Walk), since cashpoints are not always
too plentiful in the countryside. Saying that, it's still a good idea to carry
a credit card in case of emergency; and if you're walking on your own the
same could be said for a mobile phone, despite the fact that reception
may be lost in some of the more remote or mountainous locations.
After all, when you're standing alone on the windswept cliffs at
John o'Groats or Land's End staring out to sea and contemplating life,
the universe and all that kind of stuff, you'll surely want to tell someone,
somewhere that you've just walked 1,150 miles and now you're off to
buy yourself a very large drink.

the SOUTHWEST

LAND'S END TO BATH
236 miles/380km

LAND'S END TO ST BREWARD
77.5 miles/125km
ST BREWARD TO TIVERTON
80.5 miles/130km
TIVERTON TO BATH
78 miles/125km

The South West peninsula of England is generally a very attractive place
to walk, boasting a mild climate and scenery that ranges from wild
moorland to plunging cliff paths and golden bays. But for the End to
Ender striding off purposefully and perhaps a little nervously from
Land's End there is a dilemma.

The South West Coast Path is the obvious and only choice of route if
you're set on a waymarked and well-walked trail; and yet the factors that
make it so breathtaking also make it one of the most arduous paths of all.
From the moment you leave the First & Last House behind it's a
succession of ups and downs, with rough cliff tracks and plenty of steps.
If you're already fit and your feet and legs are strong then the north coast
path to Minehead is a fantastic beginning to the Walk - and it's outlined
as one of the first Alternative Routes at the end of the chapter.
Otherwise I suggest that you take it reasonably gently to begin with and
heed the direction of the main End to End route: a few coastal miles early
on, then a direct cross-country passage north-eastwards. Of course, any
route through Cornwall and Devon is never destined to be totally flat;
and the crossing of Bodmin Moor includes the two highest points in
Cornwall and some fairly rough terrain. But don't lose sight of the fact
that you have a long way to go if you want to reach the north of Scotland
and an even, measured start is probably the most sensible option if this is
your first super-long walk.

Beyond Truro the End to End route follows a straightforward and
mostly central line through the South West. However, there are relatively
few cohesive west-east trails, and in Cornwall especially rights of way
well inland from the coast path are often little-walked and sometimes
unreliable, so in some places the End to End route relies on the
ubiquitous country lane (usually direct, deserted and scenic). A few local
footpaths are used where practical, and some waymarked routes do come
into play: a day or so of the South West Coast Path, then later on the
Camel Trail near Bodmin and the Two Castles Trail from Launceston to
Okehampton. Very short sections of the Tarka Trail and Exe Valley Way
come in handy, but since both these are essentially north-south routes
neither are much use for long. At Tiverton the towpath of the former
Grand Western Canal provides an easy link to Taunton, and from here the
landscape begins to change noticeably with the Somerset Levels
giving way to the rolling Mendip Hills.

Finally, mention should be made of a couple of other interesting walking
routes through the South West that offer further End to End options.
The Land's End Trail is being developed by members of the Ramblers'
Association from Cornwall, and seeks to link Land's End with the
Ridgeway and Cotswold Way National Trails. It's an inland route that

uses local footpaths wherever possible and steers clear of most towns; and inevitably in a few places it's coincident with the route outlined in this book (such as on Bodmin Moor). However, the Land's End Trail gives two options for the crossing of Dartmoor, then links with Exmoor via the Tarka Trail. The other End to End option is the Celtic Way, a long and rather wandering route through the South West (and South Wales, too) that seeks to visit sites associated with Celtic and Neolithic history and Arthurian legend. Details of guides to both routes are given at the end of this book.

LAND'S END TO ST BREWARD
77.5 miles/125km

LAND'S END ▶ **PENZANCE YH**
11 miles/18km
PENZANCE YH ▶ **HELSTON**
17 miles/27km
HELSTON ▶ **TRURO**
17 miles/27km
TRURO ▶ **INDIAN QUEENS**
13.5miles/22km
INDIAN QUEENS ▶ **ST BREWARD**
19 miles/30km

▲ *Youth Hostel*

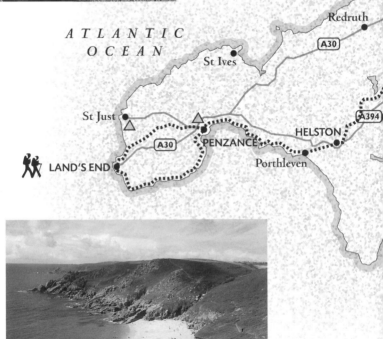

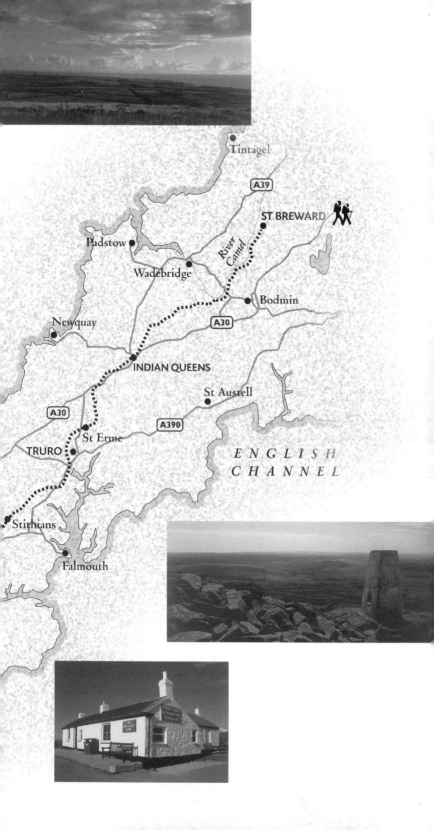

Tintagel

A39

ST BREWARD

Padstow

River Camel

Wadebridge

Bodmin

Newquay

A30

INDIAN QUEENS

St Austell

A30

A390

St Erme

TRURO

ENGLISH CHANNEL

Stithians

Falmouth

ST BREWARD TO TIVERTON
80.5 miles/130km

St Breward ▶ **Launceston**
22.5 miles/36km
Launceston ▶ **Bridestow**
17 miles/27km
Bridestow ▶ **South Zeal**
12 miles/19km
South Zeal ▶ **Crediton**
14.5 miles/23km
Crediton ▶ **Tiverton**
14.5 miles/23km

▲ *Youth Hostel*

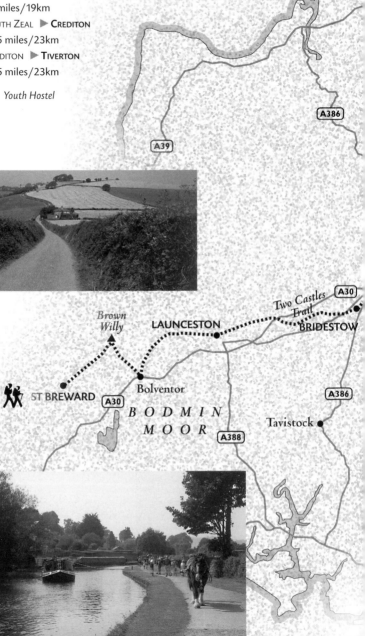

TIVERTON

A361

River Exe

A3072   A377

Yeoford   CREDITON   Thorverton

Spreyton   M5

SOUTH ZEAL   A377

A30

Okehampton   Exeter

DARTMOOR

Devon

TIVERTON TO BATH
78 miles/125km

TIVERTON ▶ **TAUNTON**
24 miles/39km
TAUNTON ▶ **STREET YH**
22 miles/35km
STREET YH ▶ **MIDSOMER NORTON**
16 miles/26km
MIDSOMER NORTON ▶ **BATH**
16 miles/26km

▲ *Youth Hostel*

B R I S T O L
C H A N N E L

M5

Quantock Hills

Bridgwater

Somerset Levels

TAUNTON

Grand Western Canal

● Wellington

A361

 TIVERTON ●

M5

A303

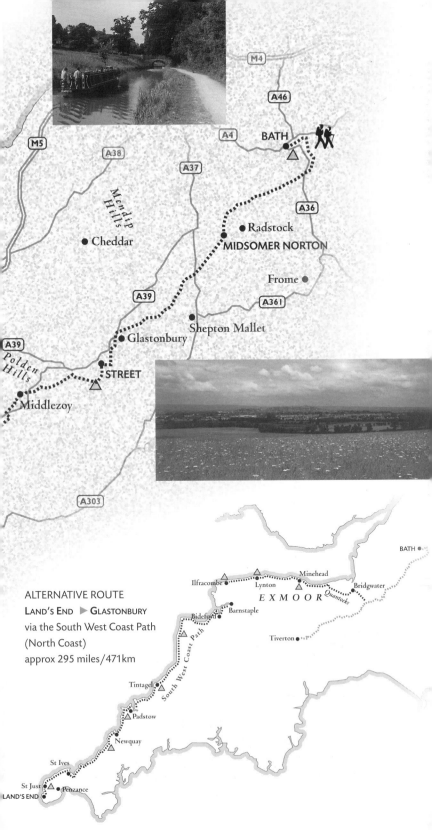

M4

A46

A4 BATH

M5

A38

A37

Mendip Hills

A36

● Radstock

MIDSOMER NORTON

● Cheddar

Frome ●

A39

A361

Shepton Mallet

A39

● Glastonbury

Polden Hills

STREET

● Middlezoy

A303

BATH ●

Minehead

Ilfracombe ●   Lynton   Bridgwater ●

EXMOOR   *Quantocks*

Bideford ●   ● Barnstaple

ALTERNATIVE ROUTE

LAND'S END ▶ GLASTONBURY

via the South West Coast Path
(North Coast)
approx 295 miles/471km

Tiverton ●

Tintagel ●

South West Coast Path

● Padstow

Newquay

St Ives

St Just

Penzance

LAND'S END

LAND'S END ▶ **PENZANCE YH,** 11 miles/18km (inland route)
16 miles/26km (coastal route)

An early start from Land's End is probably a good idea, if only to dodge
the crowds who flock to the mini theme park and wander aimlessly around
the dramatic clifftop. Nearby accommodation ranges from a campsite at
Trevescan and B&B at Sennen to the youth hostel near St Just, about
4 miles/6km away. The Land's End Hotel also offers a special rate to
prospective End to Enders (enquire beforehand). But just before you take
your first step in earnest there are a couple of things you might consider
doing: register your walk at the on-site post office or hotel reception in
order to qualify for a certificate and a chance to join the End to End Club
(see address in Chapter 7); and pose for a photo by the famous signpost -
you can choose what you want the sign to say since the actual letters are
interchangeable. There's also the 'Miles of Memories' exhibition detailing
End to End efforts over the years using various and sometimes bizarre
means of transportation. 'Walk from Land's End to John o'Groats in less
than 30 minutes' the sign outside says. I'm afraid it might take you a little
longer...

So which way are you going to head? The coast path north via Cape Cornwall
is covered by the Alternative Route section later on in the chapter, so there
are two main choices here: the south coast versus inland; the exciting,
16-mile/26km roller-coaster cliff path or the gentle, 11-mile/18km inland route
to Penzance. On a fine day the coast path is sublime, with huge soaring cliffs
overlooking minute sandy bays. Its unspoilt remoteness makes it a haven for all
sorts of wildlife, from seabirds like cormorants, gannets and shearwaters to
insects and butterflies attracted by its southerly location and sloping banks of
heather and gorse. Re-walking the path in summer 2000 I was lucky enough to
see buzzards and a peregrine falcon, and in the dazzling blue sea there
were bobbing seals and even a basking shark which had come close in to feed.
The coast path passes a handful of tiny villages and hamlets (Porthgwarra,
Porthcurno, Penberth, Lamorna) where there are refreshments in season,
but it isn't until Mousehole that there is any serious respite; and it has to be said
that rough weather will make this is an even tougher if exhilarating route.

The inland option is shorter and far easier. First, a mile of clifftop north to
Sennen Cove, then leaving the back of Whitesand Bay head east for the small
but distinctive hilly outline of Chapel Carn Brea. 'Carn Brea' means hill of stone
or rock in Cornish, and by the Bronze Age summit cairn there are splendid views
of Land's End and (if it's clear) the Scilly Isles. The National Trust sign says you
will have climbed the most westerly hill in England, although its 650ft/198m is
hardly taxing! Opposite the car park a bridleway leads to Carn Euny, a neatly
excavated Iron Age village with a 65ft/20m fogou - a long, covered chamber.
West Cornwall is rich in prehistoric remains, and should this be of particular

interest to you consider adapting your route north of Penzance to pay a visit to the fascinating ancient village of Chysauster, with its tiny stone houses and terraced gardens, and what's claimed to be oldest identifiable street in England. Beyond Sancreed there are quiet, surfaced lanes via Tremethick Cross, then footpaths down to Penzance Youth Hostel at Castle Horneck (and there's also a campsite in its grounds).

Penzance TIC: tel 01736 362207. Penzance YH: 01736 362666

 PENZANCE YH ▶ HELSTON, 17 miles/27km

Penzance is a busy regional centre, whose sea-faring heritage is reflected in attractions such as the Trinity House National Lighthouse Museum. This is the point of departure for the Scilly Isles (hence the regular helicopter flights that buzz overhead), but most of the remaining fishing fleet is based at nearby Newlyn. The coast path provides the route for most of Day Two, and by and large it's fairly straightforward. The early part along the flat shoreline of Mount's Bay is dominated by views of St Michael's Mount, a spectacular granite crag topped by a medieval castle that can be reached by a causeway at low tide and by ferry in the summer months.

Despite a short inland section up the main street of Marazion the rest of the trail sticks pretty much to the coastline, although there are a few waymarked diversions where the low, crumbly cliffs have fallen away. Beyond Cudden Point is Prussia Cove, named after local smuggler John Carter, alias the King of Prussia, who operated from this hidden spot; and from now on the views eastwards are dominated by the Lizard Peninsula stretching out into the sea. There are usually refreshments to be had at Sydney Cove, with the long golden sweep of Praa Sands before it. If you're not tempted to join the sunbathers or surfers continue along the beach itself before steps lead up towards Rinsey Head and a short but undulating section to Porthleven. The huge cliffs are breathtaking in every sense, which makes the sight of former engine houses perched precariously on the clifftop even more amazing. Wheal Prosper, a mid-19th century tin and copper mine which is on the path itself, has been restored by the National Trust.

As you descend to Porthleven you pass a memorial cross to commemorate 'mariners drowned on this part of the coast from time immemorial', and the passing of Gryll's Act in 1808 which allowed for bodies washed up from the sea to be buried in the nearest consecrated ground. Porthleven is a pleasant little place where massive catches of pilchard were once landed (the shoals could be up to 15 miles/39km square!), although today's small craft mainly fish for crab, lobster and crayfish. Sadly this is the point where you wave goodbye to the sea, and if you stay faithful to the End to End route outlined in the following

pages you won't meet the coast proper again until the north of Scotland!
So if you want to remain on the coast overnight there are some B&Bs;
otherwise back lanes take you the couple of miles into Helston.

Helston TIC: tel 01326 565431

 HELSTON ▶ TRURO, 17 miles/27km

As with so many other towns in the area Helston's origins lie in the tin
and copper industry. It was originally tidal, so exports could have been
shipped directly out, but the Loe Bar cut off the River Cober many
centuries ago - and was also responsible for the wrecking of HMS Anson
in 1807, whose impressive cannon now rests outside the back of the
Guildhall. Incidentally, this tragic event with the loss of over 100 lives
inspired Henry Trengrouse to come up with a new lifesaving rocket device
called the breeches buoy. Helston is also famous for its Flora or
Furry Dance, a day-long series of dances and merry-making in an ancient
spring festival that occurs each year on 8 May (but not Sundays
or Mondays).

From now on it's inland through Cornwall, and for the next three days that
means a network of short footpaths and country lanes. From Helston the route
assumes a north-easterly direction along a series of lanes via hamlets and
villages with splendid names like Boderwennack, Hendra, Porkellis and Carnkie.
It's an obvious enough course, and I suggest you sit down with the OS Explorer
map for a few minutes the night before and scrutinise or perhaps mark the
actual route. There are a few connecting footpaths and bridleways, especially
across Rame Common beyond Carnkie to reach Stithians, where there are pubs
and shops. The rest of the way to Truro is along any combination of country
lanes, passing numerous hamlets and attractive old farms - several of which
sport Camping & Caravanning Club accredited sites. I've measured the route via
Trebost, Frogpool, Greensplat, Quenchwell, Playing Place and Calenick - but you
could equally enter the tiny city from the west from Bissoe and Baldhu.
Just remember to consult your map at the necessary junctions, since signposts
have a curious habit of disappearing in these out-of-the-way rural places and
it is quite easy to get lost.

Considered by many to be Cornwall's true county centre, Truro is as
bustling and lively as you would expect, its sheltered position dominated
by the graceful shapes of the first Anglican cathedral to be built since
St Paul's. But it is Truro's waterside position that explains its early rise,
located at the tidal head of the River Truro which downstream becomes
the Fal and flows out into the English Channel at Falmouth.
Since medieval times Truro, like Helston, was an official coinage or

stannary town, where locally mined smelted tin had to be brought to be tested for quality and taxed.

Truro TIC: tel 01872 274555

 Truro ▶ **Indian Queens**, 13.5 miles/22km

Leave Truro by lanes either side of the River Allen, then beyond Idless turn right into Idless Wood (given as St Clement Woods on OS maps) at the car park and picnic site. It's owned by the Forestry Commission who allow access on foot. A noticeboard confirms your route: follow the lowest track along the southern edge of the woodland past the site of former gunpowder works, and also a circular Iron Age hillfort hidden further up the forested hillside, until eventually you arrive at Lanner Mill at the far northern edge of the woods. Turn right on to the lane and cross the new St Erme by-pass (A39). Skirt the southern side of the village and then take a series of often sunken, high-hedged lanes east via Boswiddle, then north towards Mitchell. Just before you enter the village turn right and going parallel with the A30 make for Summercourt. Beyond the crossroads a lane takes you high above the main road to St Enoder, after which you should follow the long straight road through Fraddon and Indian Queens.

It's not the prettiest place in Cornwall, it has to be said, but that's largely a reflection of the nearby china clay mines, which remain a crucial local employer and one of Cornwall's few surviving industries. China clay or kaolin was first used in the making of porcelain, but today its main destination is the paper industry. Its excavation produces vast pits and enormous, pale waste mounds of clay and quartze, and although some of it has recently been re-landscaped the area north of St Austell was once dubbed the 'Cornish Alps.' Indian Queens has shops and pubs, and the dubious attraction of 'Gnome World: Touring Park, Farm Shop and Gnome Park'; and camping facilities are also available a little further on at the C&C Club approved Brentons Farm. But should you feel like continuing to the hillfort at Castle-an-Dinas (and so reducing tomorrow's mileage in the process) there is farmhouse B&B and camping available at locations beyond.

Newquay TIC: tel 01637 854020

 Indian Queens ▶ **St Breward**, 19 miles/30km

From Indian Queens continue along the road past the Screech Owl Sanctuary to Castle-an-Dinas, a small but prominent hill topped by the wide grassy ramparts of an Iron Age fort. The hill also sports some Bronze Age barrows, and has latterly been the site of tin and wolfram mining. From the top there are terrific views in all directions, including the china clay 'mountains', St Breock Downs and the north Cornwall coast. Legend has it that Castle-an-Dinas was a seat of the Dark Ages dukes or petty kings of Cornwall from the 5-10th centuries AD, and that Goss Moor which lies immediately to the south was the hunting ground of King Arthur.

The footpath continues down the opposite, northern side of the hill, then strikes east to join the lane to Tregonetha. From here there's a path to St Wenn, after which it's straightforward lanes past Treliver, Tregolis, Tregustick and Tregawne - the common Cornish prefixes 'tre', 'trev' and 'treth' denote farmstead or village. Along the way you briefly meet the Saints Way, a 26-mile/42km coast to coast trail from Padstow to Fowey. Continue through Ruthernbridge to Nanstallon, at which point you join the Camel Trail at Boscarne Junction. This is the western terminus of the Bodmin & Wenford steam railway, and indeed the town of Bodmin is only a couple of miles distant should you need to divert for trips to the supermarket, chemist, bookshop, or whatever.

Fortunately the steam engines don't go any further, and the trackbed of the former Bodmin & Wadebridge Railway now hosts the Camel Trail, a popular 18-mile/29km recreational route that runs all the way from the estuary of the River Camel at Padstow via Wadebridge. In its heyday the line was used by day-trippers heading for the North Cornwall beaches, although special excursions were put on for the thousands who wanted to watch the last public hanging in Britain which occurred at Bodmin Gaol in 1909!

Today the Camel Trail caters mainly for cyclists - it forms part of the National Cycle Network Route 3 - but it's the perfect off-road route for walkers as well, easy and straightforward and very scenic. The End to End utilises the final six miles or so through shady woodland and fields before finishing at Poley's Bridge. From here it's a short distance up to the straggling hillside village of St Breward, most of which is along the route of the Camelford Way according to the latest OS Explorer map of Bodmin Moor.

Bodmin TIC: tel 01208 76616

ST BREWARD ▶ LAUNCESTON, 22.5 miles/36km

This long and potentially challenging stage involves a crossing of
Bodmin Moor via Cornwall's highest point, then a relatively
straightforward conclusion via lanes and lowland paths into Launceston.
On the face of it Bodmin Moor may seem relatively small compared to
Dartmoor but it still contains a significant area of bleak and wild
moorland where weather conditions can change quickly and navigational
expertise is essential. For End to End walkers this is a new and exciting
environment, away from civilisation if only for a while; but if the mist is
already down or bad weather is forecast a safer, alternative route is along
lanes to the north of the moors via Crowdy Reservoir.

From St Breward follow the open lane across Lady Down, then take the
waymarked public footpath via Penwood House and Lower Candra out over
King Arthur's Downs. Cairns and stone circles abound, but of more immediate
interest is a large, rectangular compound known as King Arthur's Hall.
It sits alone out on the downs, flanked by raised banks and the remains of a wall
made out of vertical stone slabs, and is presumed to have been some sort of
meeting place or site of worship. Lonely and enigmatic, it's just right for a spot
of Arthurian myth-making! The path continues until Garrow, an old farm, then
drops down to cross two wooden footbridges before skirting the flanks
of Butter's Tor and climbing directly up the slopes of Brown Willy.

On a clear day the views from Cornwall's highest point (1,377ft/420m) are
superb, the massive skyscape taking in the full sweep of the wild granite
moorland. There are man-made features such as the nearby Stannon Works
(a china clay quarry) and several stark and gleaming white wind farms; and far
beyond lies the deep blue sea with Lundy Island visible on a clear day.
Opposite Brown Willy stands Rough Tor, Cornwall's second highest peak and
crowned by more weirdly-shaped rock formations and 'clitter' (rock debris).
There's a popular path between the two hills if you've got the time to explore
or, if you prefer, you could leave St Breward by a more northerly route and take
in Rough Tor first. Otherwise, drop down the eastern slopes of Brown Willy
to the long north-south field boundary below.
This old wall runs all the way south to Tolborough Tor, on the far side of
which a walled lane leads down to Jamaica Inn next to the A30. Made famous
by the novel of Daphne Du Maurier, who stayed here in 1930, the old coaching
inn has inevitably turned into something of a tourist trap with gift shops, a
museum, and the Dame Daphne Du Maurier Memorial Room (featuring her
Sheraton writing desk and 'a dish of Glacier Mints, her favourite sweets');
but it's still a handy place to stop for a pot of tea.

From Jamaica Inn re-cross the A30 via the underpass and take the no-through
lane that turns into a public bridleway across Hendra Downs and West Moor.

At Carne Down the track descends from moorland into gentler farmland, and from here it's a succession of lanes all the way to Launceston - unless you decide to shorten the day and stay somewhere else. If not, the obvious route is via Tresmeake, Lower Tregunnon, Trethinna, Trewen and Gospenheale, then the lane that runs along the Kensey valley parallel with the Launceston Steam Railway.

Launceston TIC: tel 01566 772321

 LAUNCESTON ▶ BRIDESTOW, 17 miles/27km

From Launceston to Okehampton you will be following a short, waymarked route called the Two Castles Trail. It's pleasant and rural, through quiet river valleys and woodland, a gentle pastoral wander after the moorland yomping of yesterday; and despite the front of the guidebook claiming 30 miles it's in fact only 24 miles/39km long. This being the case you could make it to Okehampton and its youth hostel for nightfall if you start early, and so adjust the subsequent days accordingly. But much will depend on factors as varied as the weather, the state of your feet, and how rigid a timetable you have set yourself - if indeed you have in the first place.
The Two Castles Trail is not marked on OS maps at present, but the guidebook (more of a leaflet pack, actually) available from Launceston TIC includes an eastbound description and together with the waymarks it's quite easy and obvious to work out where you're going.

Launceston, the ancient capital of Cornwall, is worth an inspection first. It was the only walled town in the county, and today is dominated by the remains of what was originally a Norman castle founded by William the Conqueror's half brother who was made Earl of Cornwall. Largely disused by the 17th century it continued to hold the county assizes and prison, and George Fox, the Quakers founder, was once an inmate.

From Southgate Arch, the only remaining gate from the original town walls, the trail strikes out east to the campsite at Polson Bridge. Here you meet the River Tamar and cross from Cornwall into Devon. At last - the second county of the Walk! A path south of the River Carey and roads via Lifton leads to Dingles Steam Village, with various industrial heritage attractions; then footpaths and lanes continue via Stowford and Lewtard to Lewtrenchard, where you will also see signs for the Sabine Baring-Gould Trail.
The Rev Baring-Gould is best known for writing the hymn 'Onward Christian Soldiers', but as a typically prolific Victorian gentleman he was also a gifted linguist, collector and writer of novels and travel books. He was both village squire and parson for over 40 years, and is buried in the churchyard at Lewtrenchard.

The trail continues via Lew Mill and a permissive path across Galford Down, where the Saxons under King Egbert of Wessex defeated a Celtic uprising in AD825. There are wide views over the surrounding countryside, not least of the huge bulk of Dartmoor now drawing very close indeed. From the downs a public footpath leads around the flanks of Burley Wood below the remains of Iron Age and Norman fortifications; then a lane through Watergate takes you to Bridestowe.

Okehampton TIC: tel 01837 53020. Okehampton YH: tel 01837 53916

 Bridestow ▶ South Zeal, 12 miles/19km

From Bridestowe the Two Castles Trail continues via paths to Sourton, then follows a clear track up on to the edge of Dartmoor to pass below Sourton Tors and drop back down to a walled lane that leads to the hamlet of Meldon. But there's no need to stick to the prescribed route, of course. Despite the Ministry of Defence's range further east there's a fair amount of access land to be explored, and one of the most popular spots is nearby Meldon Reservoir. The track from the car park/picnic site near its dam leads down past Meldon viaduct - which can also be seen from the Two Castles Trail - a huge wrought iron structure 120ft/36m high that used to carry London and South Western Railway trains into Cornwall.

A glance at the latest Explorer map (113: Okekampton) will show that from Sourton the TCT's route has also been shared by the West Devon Way, which runs from Plymouth to Okehampton via Tavistock and the western edge of Dartmoor National Park. Both routes cross above the A30 and enter Okehampton via the relative peace of its golf course, while over the river on your left are the ruins of the Normans' Okehampton Castle.

Okehampton itself is a handy place to re-stock on provisions, and the Museum of Dartmoor Life, housed in a 19th century mill, is worth a visit. Just round the corner is a mountain rescue post, which gives you some indication of the terrain that lies only a few miles away in the National Park.

The final 7.5 miles/12km from Okehampton to South Zeal are very pleasant, wandering alongside small river valleys and rolling fields, and with the bulky outline of Dartmoor high above to the south. Most of this section is along the Tarka Trail, a 181-mile/291km route that follows the journeys of Tarka the Otter and takes in locations featured in Henry Williamson's well-known book. This is one adventurous and clever otter, since the large figure-of-eight route ranges from Barnstaple to Ilfracombe and Lynton, and inland to Okehampton via a railway connection! However, the End to End route only follows the

Tarka Trail as far as Sticklepath; so from Okehampton look out for the otter pawprint waymarks and head along the valley of the East Okement River for a short distance, then via field paths and lanes to Belstone. From here the route shadows the River Taw to Sticklepath before heading north, while you should continue another mile to use the overnight facilities at South Zeal. And if you arrive early why not drop your pack at the campsite and stretch your legs - Cosdon Hill is only the small matter of 1,800ft/550m above, and enjoys fine views over northern Dartmoor.

Okehampton TIC: tel 01837 53020. Okehampton YH: tel 01837 53916

 SOUTH ZEAL ▶ CREDITON, 14.5 miles/23km

Mid Devon has a number of good walking trails, but most of them are north-south (Two Moors Way, Tarka Trail, Exe Valley Way) or too short (Taw-Teign Link, Little Dart Ridge and Valley Walk) to be of much use in the great End to End scheme of things. This is why from South Tawton, a short stroll away from the day's start at South Zeal, most of this stage is along peaceful country roads and farm tracks. The deep, winding lanes see very little traffic, and many of the thatched hamlets and villages you pass through are unspoilt and delightful. There are a few decent views, particularly when you near the Yeo valley, and plenty of wildlife in the thick, high hedges, which act as mini nature reserves in their own right. But shops and general amenities are not especially plentiful, so either time your visit to the Foal & Mare pub at Yeoford accordingly or make sure you're well supplied.

From South Tawton the most obvious, direct route is via Langdown and Spreyton all the way east to Yeoford. For a while above the River Troney you share the lane with the Two Moors Way, a 102-mile/164km cross-Devon route from Ivybridge on the Channel coast to Lynmouth on the Exmoor shore. Around Yeoford you'll no doubt notice the startlingly red earth along the lower edges of the lanes and in the ploughed fields, plus the red sandstone that make some of the older buildings so distinctive. Beyond the village the lanes become rather more undulating and lead directly into Crediton, a prosperous medieval wool town that was in fact the See of the first bishopric in Devon, until it moved to Exeter in the 11th century. Crediton is also believed to have been the birthplace of Windfrith, better known as St Boniface, in AD680, one of the most renown Christian missionaries and patron saint of both Germany and The Netherlands.

Crediton TIC: tel 01363 772006

CREDITON ▶ **TIVERTON**, 14.5 miles/23km

Leave Crediton by footpath eastwards across Lord's Meadows to reach
Shobrooke, after which the lane continues directly to the handsome village of
Thorverton with its colourful borders and neat buildings (and, more practically,
a shop and a couple of pubs). Here you join the Exe Valley Way that traces
the route of the River Exe for 45-miles/72 km from its source at Hawkridge on
Exmoor to its estuary south of Exeter. The End to End follows the trail
northwards for 8 miles/13km as far as Tiverton, and includes a glorious final
riverside stretch from Bickleigh. For the first few miles the waymarked trail sticks
to the lane north from Thorverton, as it dips and rises to reveal wonderful views
over the Exe valley below, then descends rapidly to Bickleigh Bridge.
On your left is Bickleigh Castle, a fortified medieval manor house described by
its owners as a 'Royalist stronghold spanning 900 years of History'; then cross
the river by the historic five-arched bridge - purportedly the inspiration behind
Simon and Garfunkel's song 'Bridge over Troubled Water'! At the touristy
Bickleigh Mill turn left for the path up the quiet east bank all the way into
Tiverton. For much of the way this peaceful route enjoys the shelter of wildlife-
rich woodland, mainly oak and ash, but beware some waterlogged conditions
after heavy rain.

The noise and bustle of Tiverton comes as something of a shock,
although the modern facade you see today disguises the fact that the town
is of Anglo Saxon origin. Its most prosperous time was in the 17th and
18th centuries when it was a major centre for the cloth industry.
At one time there were over 50 mills in the area producing the famous
'kersey', a coarse woollen worsted in red, blue and green dyes.

Tiverton TIC: tel 01884 255827

TIVERTON ▶ TAUNTON, 24 miles/39km

In terms of walking conditions your progress through the South West
(or West Country) so far has been quite varied: coastal trail, moorland tracks,
field paths, country lanes, riverside - and now it's the turn of canal towpath.
The 24 miles/39km of the Grand Western Canal to Taunton are, as you would
expect, flat and easy, although most of the eastern section has reverted to
footpaths since the actual canal has disappeared. But if the distance is too much
there are a couple of campsites near Wellington and scattered B&Bs that can
easily make for a shorter day.

The story of the Grand Western Canal is fascinating, since it was
originally intended to form part of an ambitious project to link the
Bristol and English Channels and so cut out the hazardous sea journey
around Land's End. But of course canal-building was a long and expensive
exercise, and eventually the plans foundered due to indecision, rising
costs and wage bills, plus the emergence of the railways, so that only this
short section of the canal between Tiverton and Taunton was ever built.
Today the Devon section of the canal (11 miles/18km) is run by
the county council as a country park, and at the basin at Tiverton there's
a canal shop, seasonal floating tearoom, and even trips on a horse-drawn
barge. Below the canal are some former lime kilns, since this important
agricultural commodity was much in demand in the 19th century to
improve the poor Devon soils.

Before long you're striding clear of Tiverton and waterside progress is quiet and
easy. The small aqueduct once carried the canal over a branch of the
Bristol & Exeter Railway - itself now consigned to history. The canal meanders
as it maintains its level course along the contour (hence no need for locks),
passing successive milestones as it does so. It runs through the middle of
Sampford Peverell and for a while is parallel with the M5 before heading north
past Canonsleigh Priory to briefly disappear into Waytown Tunnel and reach
the Somerset border at Lowdwells Lock, east of Holcumbe Regis.

Unfortunately the remaining distance to Taunton (about 13 miles/21km)
is along the course of the former canal, although as you will see the paths and
tracks stick very close to the original route and sometimes even assumes the dry
bed of the original waterway. A few short sections of the old canal are marked
on the OS map (although there are detailed walking guides available), and some
relics also remain, including the ruins of the Lift at Nynehead which raised the
boats 24 ft/7m. But for much of the way into Taunton you shadow the River
Tone, around the edges of Wellington, Bradford-on-Tone
and Norton Fitzwarren.

Taunton TIC: tel 01823 336344

Taunton ▶ **Street YH**, 22 miles/35km

For much of the Middle Ages the county town of Somerset owed its
prosperity to wool, and it was this that financed Taunton's great church
tower (which, incidentally, was deemed unsafe and taken down in 1858,
only to be rebuilt exactly as before). The River Tone runs through the
town centre, and ahead there are more horizontal waterside miles as gentle,
rolling farmland gives way to the unique landscape of the Somerset Levels
and Moors. It's another long stage, but again relatively easy.

Walk the towpath of the Bridgwater & Taunton Canal out of the town centre
eastwards from Firepool Lock via Bathpool and Creech St Michael. Leave at
Bridge 13, near Charlton, and cross the railway to join the River Tone.
The raised embankment leads all the way to Burrowbridge, which is dominated
by the ruined, hilltop chapel of Burrow Mump; and from the willow craft centre
and hurdle-makers at Curload the waterside route is also shared by the
River Parrett Trail, which runs for a total of 50 miles/80 km from the hills of
Dorset to the river's mouth in Bridgwater Bay.

This flat and unique area of wetlands was once the floodplain of five
rivers, the deposits of which formed a coastal plain (the Levels) which in
turn caused inland marsh and bog (the Moors). Since it is only a few feet
above sea level regular flooding has always been a feature of this landscape,
but over the centuries the farming value of the land has led to ever-more
sophisticated attempts at drainage: hundreds of channels or 'rhynes'
have been cut across the wetlands, river banks straightened, and sluices
and pumping houses have been constructed. But this in turn has
posed environmental dilemmas, since the wetlands' peculiar natural
habitat (it's home to rare dragonflies, otters and birds like lapwing and
snipe) only survives through frequent, natural flooding.

Walking between Burrowbridge and Street is complicated by the maze of
criss-crossing drainage ditches; and by the fact that this location falls on the
boundary of three different Explorer maps! You could head south east on lanes
to Aller and the lumpy hilltop of High Ham, then go north across Walton Moor
to Street. However, the End to End route opts for quiet lanes to Middlezoy, then
after a short burst of the A361 turns right at Greylake Bridge to follow King
Sedgemoor's Drain as far as Cradle Bridge. Go north along the road until Nythe,
then take the lane east across Butleigh Moor to Walton Hill. From the top of
this long ridge (known as the Polden Hills) there are great views back across the
Levels to High Ham and Dundon Hill. Turn the other way and there is
the equally enticing vista of Glastonbury Tor and the Mendip Hills. And, since
this is National Trust land, there's a pleasant, off-road track along the hilltop
all the way to Street Youth Hostel at Ivy Thorn Hill.

Glastonbury TIC: tel 01458 832954. Street YH: tel 01458 442961

STREET YH ▶ MIDSOMER NORTON, 16 miles/26km

From Street Youth Hostel it is roughly 32 miles/51km until Bath,
which is almost certainly too much to walk in one day, especially as the
Mendip Hills lie in between. However, if you extend the previous stage a
little and stay at Glastonbury or even Wells (and there are plenty of B&Bs
and campsites) you could lessen the overall distance; and at the conclusion
of the stage you could also chip a few miles off by ignoring the
Kennet & Avon Canal Path loop and heading directly for Bath Youth
Hostel. There's also plenty of scope to fashion your own route if you
wanted to visit Cheddar Gorge or the glorious Wells Cathedral, both of
which are a little to the west of the main End to End passage.

It's a short roadside walk into Glastonbury from Street, and whatever you may
think of the hype surrounding King Arthur and the Isle of Avalon there's no
getting away from the magnetism of Glastonbury Tor (nor the excellent views
from the top). Legend says that Joseph of Arimathea buried the chalice used at
the Last Supper underneath the hill, and that the long-vanished abbey that gave
rise to the present town was the first site of Christianity in Britain.
To reach the Mendips proper cross the last of the Levels north of Glastonbury.
From Hartlake Bridge there's a public footpath along Twelve Foot Rhyne; but
more direct is Long Drove, a dead-straight lane along Long Drove Rhyne to
Launcherly. If you keep your eyes open you'll notice occasional stone sculptures
by the roadside which in fact act as markers and milestones, since this is also the
route of the National Cycle Network's Route 3. It's also evident approaching
Dulcote, where there's a handy pedestrian/cycle tunnel under the new A371 by-
pass. After paths from Dulcote through Dinder follow the rising Sleight and
Crapnell Lanes to reach Maesbury Castle at the far end.
There are good views across the Mendips from the high grassy embankments of
this ancient fort, a location thankfully free of scruffy car parks or vandalised
noticeboards, after which it's a descent across the golf course to reach
Gurney Slade by back roads. Scuttling quickly over the A37 and past the quarry
entrance you can either take wooded tracks around Blacker's Hill or tarmac via
Chilcompton to pick up one of the long, direct lanes into Midsomer Norton.

MIDSOMER NORTON ▶ BATH, 16 miles/26km

One of the most attractive features of Midsomer Norton is the river
that runs down the main street - you may remember that Helston
in Cornwall also posed pedestrians a similar if lesser problem with its
watery gutters. To the east the old market town merges into Radstock, a
former mining and railway centre that grew up on the relatively little-
known North Somerset Coalfield, and whose output played a significant
part in powering the Industrial Revolution in Bath and Bristol.

From Midsomer there are lanes directly to the village of Radford a couple
of miles away, and here you pick up the Limestone Link Path. It's waymarked by
an ammonite fossil logo, as well as being usefully indicated on the latest
Explorer maps, and connects the West Mendip Way at Shipham with the
Cotswold Way at Cold Ashton. For now it's mainly field paths, riverbank and
shady lanes as you follow the north-easterly course of Cam Brook, a pleasant
little stream that threads its way between the hills via the villages of Camerton,
Dunkerton, Combe Hay and Monkton Combe. Finally you arrive at a larger
valley where almost every conceivable manner of transport route is represented:
river (Avon), road (A36), canal (Kennet & Avon), railway (Bath branch line) and
walking trail (Avon Walkway, Kennet & Avon Canal Walk).

Now, if you just want to head directly for Bath Youth Hostel leave the
Limestone Link Path at Monkton Combe and head uphill to Claverton Down,
around the edge of which runs the National Trust's six-mile 'Bath Skyline'
circular walk across fields and through parkland. There are local signs and maps,
but essentially make for Rainbow Wood Farm and the university, from where
the youth hostel on Bathwick Hill is only a few minutes' walk away.
However, assuming that this is a relatively short day - and there is plenty
to see once you reach Bath, of course - the easier and more unhurried
(although longer) entrance to Bath is to follow the Kennet & Avon Canal
towpath as both it and the River Avon wind their way around the foot of the
wooded Bathampton Down into the city centre. But first of all enjoy
a well-deserved cuppa at Brass Knocker Basin, the modern and bustling canal
centre just off the A36. There is information on the restored Somerset Coal
Canal, the Dundas Aqueduct (which you pass shortly) and the Kennet & Avon
Canal whose Reading-Bristol route is once more attracting visitors - both on
the water and on the bank. In fact the 84-mile/135km route is now a recognised
walking trail, and together with the local Avon Walkway and the Bristol & Bath
Railway Path the off-road choice for walkers is extensive.

Bath TIC: tel 01225 477101. Bath YH: tel 01225 465674

LAND'S END ▶ **GLASTONBURY**
via the South West Coast Path (north coast)
approx 295 miles/471km

Coastal paths don't get any better than this; nor any tougher. In total
the South West Coast Path National Trail stretches 600 miles/966km around
the shores of Dorset, Devon, Cornwall and Somerset, and which ever way you
head from Land's End - north coast or south - the scenery is wonderfully varied
but often exacting. High headlands and towering cliffs contrast with sheltered
coves and wide sandy bays; while picturesque fishing villages vie with brash
resorts and vast caravan parks. Bearing in mind that most of the End to End
route is inland this is the best chance to enjoy some top drawer coastal scenery,
and if this is your goal there are two options.

In the past a few End to Enders have followed the south coast to Plymouth
(and then inland via Dartmoor); or even on to somewhere like Lyme Regis
before striking northwards. But the most logical route is along the north coast
via St Ives, Padstow, Bude and Bideford, with a short cut from Barnstaple across
Exmoor an obvious possibility. The coast path's northern terminus is at
Minehead, in north Somerset, and from here to Street or Glastonbury it's quite
a straightforward two or possibly three-day walk: coastal access continues as far
as Watchet, then local paths take you over the Quantock Hills to Bridgwater.
After this it's the Somerset Levels, where you can pick up the main End to End
route at Middlezoy or High Ham.

The South West Coast Path is waymarked and well-walked, and apart from
the occasional cliff-fall or confusion through a town centre it's not difficult to
follow. There are plenty of places to stay and campsites are abundant, although
it can get tight at the really popular spots; but in any event if you carry a copy of
the South West Coast Path Association's annual handbook and directory you
shouldn't go far wrong (see Chapter 7). As with the Pembrokeshire Coast Path
in South West Wales, it's heavenly to walk along on a sunny spring or summer's
morning when the wild flowers are out and the birds and insects are wheeling in
the sky; but, on the flipside, there's no greater struggle than when the wind and
rain lashes in from the Atlantic and you're forced to walk almost doubled-up.
So be suitably prepared!

the *SEVERN & MIDLANDS*

BATH TO EDALE
238 miles/383km

BATH TO TEWKESBURY
89.5 miles/144km
TEWKESBURY TO PENKRIDGE
87.5 miles/141km
PENKRIDGE TO EDALE
61.5 miles/99km

After your long trek through the peninsula of South West England it's now time to swing north, and into the heart of the land. This is a fascinating section of gentle contrasts, and of gradual but ongoing change: accents begin to alter (from the distinctive West Country 'burr' to the flatter vowels of the Black Country); there are more extensive tracts of woodland; and after a largely rural passage through Cornwall, Devon and Somerset you gradually become aware that large urban centres are now quite close. From the centre of Bath the Cotswold Way offers several days of sustained if modest elevation, pretty village scenes and fabulous views over Cheltenham and Gloucester towards Wales; then after a short burst of the Gloucestershire Way it's down to the Severn Way for some pleasant riverside miles via historic Tewkesbury and Worcester.

Next, the Worcestershire Way picks up the baton for less than a day, before passing it to the Staffordshire Way in order to steer a green path to the west of the West Midlands urban sprawl, and taking in canal towpaths, stately homes and the delightful pocket of heathland that is Cannock Chase. But before long the mild farmland of Staffordshire gives way to the more rugged hills of Derbyshire, and the Limestone Way is your guide through the southern reaches of the Peak District. Now you're entering some serious hill country, with the scenery and sometimes the weather to match, and you'll see more walkers and backpackers like yourself. And, as you approach Castleton and Edale, the mighty Pennine chain heaves into view, and the End to End Walk pulls up its socks and gets serious.

As far as the practicalities are concerned, most of this section follows long distance footpaths that are not only described in detail in individual guide books, but their routes are also shown on OS Explorer or Outdoor Leisure maps. What could be simpler! Even better, they are all waymarked on the ground, either by the usual finger posts or eye-catching symbols - the National Trail acorn (Cotswold Way), a sailing boat (Severn Way), a Worcestershire pear and Staffordshire knot, and the curled horns of a ram's head for the Limestone Way. But, as ever, don't expect a sign at every stile.

Now that you're entering the second section of the Walk there are also more and more options for alternative routes. Two of the main ones are outlined - the Offa's Dyke Path along the Welsh Borders and across the Cheshire Plain to the Pennines, and the Heart of England Way through Warwickshire and the countryside east of Birmingham. But there are other variations possible: you could miss out the Cotswolds by joining the Severn Way from its start near Bristol, and then continue further along to Shrewsbury, before heading north towards Cheshire along the Shropshire Way. Alternatively if you stuck to the Staffordshire Way until just beyond Leek you could pick up the Gritstone Trail and enter the Dark Peak from the west. Decisions, decisions.

The Devil's Chimney, Cotswold Way

BATH TO TEWKESBURY
89.5 miles/144km

BATH ▶ **TOMARTON**
16 miles/26km
TOMARTON ▶ **DURSLEY**
19 miles/30km
DURSLEY ▶ **PAINSWICK**
14.5 miles/23km
PAINSWICK ▶ **DOWDESWELL RES**
17.5 miles/28km
DOWDESWELL RES ▶ **TEWKESBURY**
22.5 miles/36km

▲ *Youth Hostel*

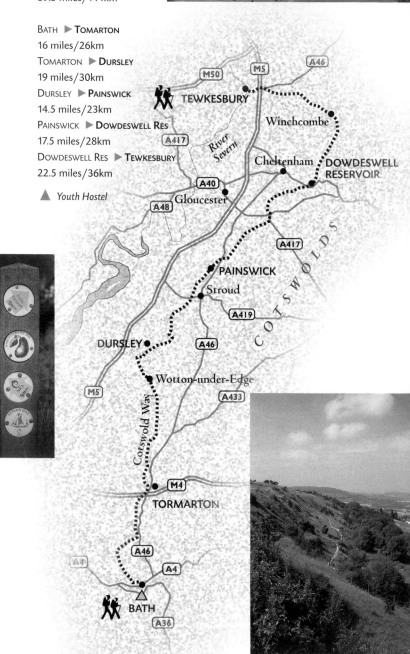

TEWKESBURY TO PENKRIDGE
87.5 miles/141km

TEWKESBURY ▶ WORCESTER
19.5 miles/31km
WORCESTER ▶ BEWDLEY
17.5 miles/28km
BEWDLEY ▶ KINVER EDGE
10.5 miles/17km
KINVER EDGE ▶ SEISDON
20.5 miles/33km
SEISDON ▶ PENKRIDGE
19.5 miles/31km

PENKRIDGE TO EDALE
61.5 miles/99km

PENKRIDGE ▶ **ABBOTS BROMLEY**
17 miles/27km
ABBOTS BROMLEY ▶ **ILAM**
20 miles/32km
ILAM ▶ **MILLER'S DALE**
15 miles/24km
MILLER'S DALE ▶ **EDALE**
9 miles/14km

▲ *Youth Hostel*

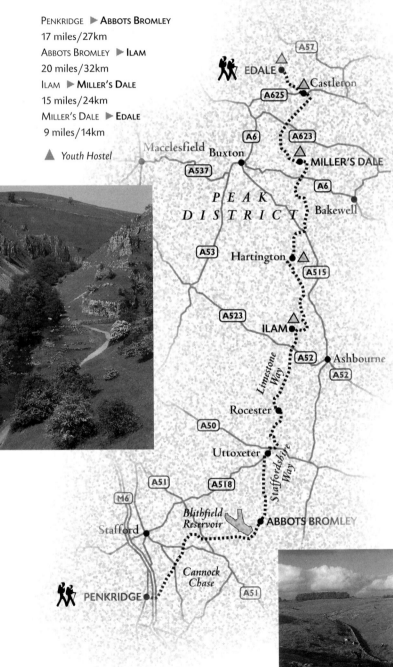

A57

🚶🚶 EDALE ▲
▲ Castleton
A625

A6 A623

A6

Macclesfield Buxton ▲ MILLER'S DALE

A537

P E A K
D I S T R I C T Bakewell

A53 Hartington ▲
A515

A523
▲
ILAM

Limestone Way A52 Ashbourne
A52

Rocester

A50

Uttoxeter

A51 A518 Staffordshire Way

M6 *Blithfield*
Reservoir **ABBOTS BROMLEY**
Stafford

Cannock
Chase
🚶🚶 PENKRIDGE A51

ALTERNATIVE ROUTE 1
BATH ▶ **CROWDEN**
via the Offa's Dyke Path
approx 261 miles/420km

ALTERNATIVE ROUTE 2
WINCHCOMBE ▶ **CANNOCK CHASE**
via the Heart of England Way
80 miles/129km

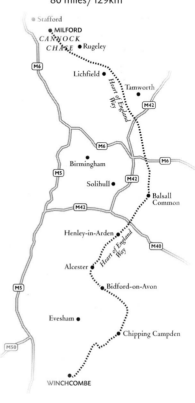

BATH ▶ TOMARTON, 16 miles/26km

Bath's enduring popularity owes much to the Romans who established
a series of spa baths and pools here. In fact they were only rediscovered in
1879, but since then visitors have flocked to the elegant Georgian terraces
and crescents, the numerous parks and gardens, so that Bath has been
designated a World Heritage City. The southern end of the Cotswold Way
begins at Bath Abbey and winds its way up through the town in a north-
westerly direction. It passes the famous Royal Crescent, a stunning piece
of architecture when seen from the open lawns below, and via path and
pavement makes for the suburb of Weston.

In its entirety the Cotswold Way runs 103 miles/166km from Bath to
Chipping Campden. The local Ramblers' Association suggested a trail along the
Cotswold escarpment as far back as 1953, but despite being 'opened' in 1970
it has only just become a fully-fledged National Trail. A number of minor route
changes have taken place over the years, mainly to avoid potentially awkward or
dangerous road crossings, and with others likely some older guidebooks may
now contain a few inaccuracies. As always, it's best to stick to the most recent
OS maps, and of course look for signs and waymarks on the ground.

Beyond Weston you reach open hillside at last, and from Penn Hill there are
views across Bath and the Avon valley. The route now keeps to the high ground,
and after skirting Bath racecourse continues rather erratically north-eastwards
to the village of Cold Ashton. After negotiating a couple of main roads
the Cotswold Way passes through Dyrham Wood to the reach the village of the
same name; and then passes around the northern perimeter of the National
Trust's Dyrham Park. In the centre of the ancient deer park is a house built
around 1700 for William Blathwayt, Secretary of State for William III. Most of its
original furnishings remain, including the distinctive blue and white delftware,
and period textiles and artwork. Well worth a brief visit for a pot of tea and
a look around.

Beyond Dyrham there are more field paths, then a short section of the A46
in order to cross the M4 at the Tormarton interchange. Tormarton itself is on
the far side, and there are also buses into nearby Chipping Sodbury.

It's probably worth pointing out that although there is plenty of B&B
accommodation in the Cotswolds generally there is not always a huge amount
on the trail itself. Campsites are few, and apart from Bath there are no youth
hostels on the trail now that Cleeve Hill has been closed. However, larger villages
and towns are never too far away (Stroud, Gloucester, Cheltenham), so it's
unlikely you'll be completely stranded. That said, it's still a good idea to pick up a
copy of the inexpensive Cotswold Way Handbook which has details of all the
local B&Bs, campsites, taxi services, and so on (see Chapter 7).

TOMARTON ▶ DURSLEY, 19 miles/30km

Across the Bath Road from Tormarton the Cotswold Way resumes through
Dodington Park, landscaped (inevitably) by Capability Brown. Beyond is
Old Sodbury, the original village (Little and Chipping Sodbury are newer) and
then Horton. Across the main street is the drive to Horton Court, a fine old
stone building which also encompasses a much older Norman hall.
Behind the manor house the route climbs the typically steep scarp slope of the
Cotswolds. In terms of elevation the hills are not particularly high (a little over
1,000 ft/300m) but the main ridge provides a good vantage point over the
Severn plain. As you will notice, the local stone is a popular building material,
since the oolitic limestone (also called 'egg stone' since it resembles
closely-packed fish eggs) is easily worked and colours well.

The next feature of note is the Somerset Monument, dedicated to General
Lord Somerset who served at Waterloo, then a little beyond this the trail heads
north-east past some lovely woodland above Long Coombe. A lane from
Lower Kilcott leads to Kilcott Mill, and from here to Alderley you keep above a
small stream and springs that gave rise to a small and short-lived pocket of
industry based on a succession of water mills. From Alderley the route heads up
the wooded slopes of Wortley Hill, then follows a lane back down and into
Wotton under Edge. This pleasant little town owed its early prosperity to the
wool trade, which manifested itself in the Dawes Almshouses, on Church Street,
and the fine parish church of St Mary's.

The Cotswold Way leaves Wotton's main street at the western end to climb
Wotton Hill and resume what is now becoming the characteristic route
along the top edge of the escarpment. In this respect I have always enjoyed
walking the Cotswold Way, with its ever-changing views and sense of elevation,
and here the panorama across the wide plain of the River Severn takes in
the outskirts of Bristol and even the towers of the two Severn bridges; but soon
they are blocked by a modern conifer plantation next to
Brackenbury Ditches (the remains of a hill fort). Out into the open again
to reach the distinctive Tyndale Monument, erected in 1866 to the memory of
William Tyndale who translated the Bible into English - and was subsequently
burnt at the stake because of it. The route drops down to North Nibley,
and nearby is Nibley Green, site of the last battle fought by private armies in
England, when Lord Berkeley and Viscount De Lisle (plus around 2000 retainers)
skirmished in 1470. Now it's a plod back up to Stinchcombe Hill, where among
the fairways and bunkers of a golf course there is the option of a short
2 mile/3km circuit around the edge of the hilltop. Worth it for the views maybe,
but at the end of quite a long day you may feel that it is time to descend to
Dursley and rest those weary feet.

Stroud TIC: tel 01453 765768

Dursley ▶ Painswick, 14.5 miles/23km

From Dursley the Cotswold Way surmounts the two small but sharp hills of
Peaked Down and Cam Long Down. If your breakfast still lies heavy in your
stomach the lane to the south is an easier option. Either way, the goal at the far
side is Uley Bury, an extensive Iron Age hill fort of long grassy ramparts and
ditches. In fact this area is rich in ancient remains, for just to the north the Way
visits first Hetty Pegler's Tump, a well-preserved long barrow; then another at
Nympsfield. They date from around 2,500BC, and when the latter's stone-built
chambers were excavated last century various items of pottery, arrowheads,
tools, plus 20-30 burials, were discovered. (Hetty Pegler was actually the name
of the wife of the 17th century owner of the field!)

From the ice cream vans and picnickers in Coaley Peak Country Park the route
continues along the hilltop to Pen Hill, then loses height via Middleyard
and the edge of King's Stanley to join a road opposite Stanley Mills, the first
industrial building in Britain to be built as a fire-proof structure, no less.
As you cross the River Frome and Stroudwater Canal the town of Stroud, with
all its amenities, is a short walk along the road to your right. It was once the
most important centre in the country for the production of broadcloth,
but nowadays many of the mill buildings have been put to other use -
Ebley Mill now houses the offices of Stroud District Council, for instance.

The Cotswold Way heads swiftly back up to the slopes above the village of
Randwick for a long and pleasant section through the trees of Standish Wood.
Like Stinchcombe Hill yesterday the route makes its way out to and around the
edge of Haresfield Hill, and although the 713ft/217m Haresfield Beacon is not
tremendously high the views across the valley of the Severn to the
Forest of Dean are nevertheless rewarding. Now the Cotswold Way ascends
the slopes of Scottsquar Hill in order to thread its way via some disused quarries
to reach the delightful village of Painswick,

Painswick is most notable for its parish churchyard that contains ninety
nine immaculately clipped yew trees, each about 200 years old.
However, the high spire on the church has had its share of misfortunes:
following Charles I's stay in the village Parliamentarian forces used the
spire as a ranging mark; and during a violent thunderstorm in 1883 a
lightning strike sent 40ft/12m of the tower crashing through the church
roof causing considerable damage.

Stroud TIC: tel 01453 765768

Painswick ▶ Dowdeswell reservoir, 17.5 miles/28km

From Painswick the Cotswold Way aims directly north via the local golf course to reach Painswick Hill and Kites Hill, and after crossing the A46 resumes its woodland path by entering Buckholt Wood, an ancient beech wood that forms part of the Cotswold Commons and Beechwoods National Nature Reserve. The pleasant tree-cover continues intermittently as far as Cooper's Hill where, on a narrow open slope, an annual cheese-rolling competition takes place each Spring Bank Holiday Monday. This famous event sees a number of brave (or possibly just plain daft) local people race down an unfeasibly steep slope in pursuit of a 7lb Double Gloucester cheese. Entrants regularly suffer minor injuries and concussion. It's believed that the peculiar custom originated as a means of reinforcing commoners' rights to graze sheep on the hillside.

Now the trail swings eastwards, above the Roman villa of Great Witcombe, and after Witcombe Wood and Birdlip Hill the route makes for Crickley Hill Country Park. The visitor centre has an interesting display on the park's older inhabitants - Neolithic settlements (3,500-2,000BC) have been excavated - and its natural attractions, including adders and birds, and a host of butterflies that enjoy the 'unimproved' (ie pesticide-free) limestone grassland.

With continuing good views over Cheltenham to the Black Mountains and the Welsh border the route turns abruptly right at Shurdington long barrow to reach Leckhampton Hill. The long-abandoned quarries that once eat into the hillside have left some curious relics: stone sleepers, from the horse-drawn tramways that were used to transport the rock and stone; and a tall column of rock known as the Devil's Chimney that the quarrymen deliberately left standing and which has now become a famous local landmark. Before it was forbidden to climb the fast-eroding Chimney, an amazing total of 13 people all managed to squeeze on to its tiny summit at once!

After some easy tracks through the scrub above Charlton Kings Common the Cotswold Way reaches Seven Springs - the source of the River Churn - where it decides to take a 2.5 mile/4km diversion south in order to cut out a 1 mile/1.5km roadside section to Wistley Hill. Hopefully a new walking route can eventually be agreed. This stage concludes at the busy A40 by Dowdeswell Reservoir, where there are regular buses into Charlton Kings and Cheltenham.

Cheltenham Spa TIC: tel 01242 522878

Dowdeswell Reservoir ▶ Tewkesbury, 22.5 miles/36km

This longish stage could be broken at Winchcombe, the convenient and attractive half-way point, which is also the spot that marks your switch from the Cotswold Way to the Gloucestershire Way. However, the continuation to Tewkesbury is not overly arduous, and perhaps the lure of finishing the day at an historic town on the banks of the River Severn may be too tempting. Plus you will have chipped off another few miles.

The Cotswold Way resumes opposite the Reservoir Inn, below Dowdeswell Reservoir, and heads north along open lanes and field paths to Cleeve Hill, the highest point on the National Trail at 1,040ft/317m. The route makes a huge circuit of Cleeve Common, a bare and windy spot that is in fact home to an important range of wild flowers and butterflies; but despite the excellent views you may be tempted to cut out the golf course and Iron Age fort if you're running late or the weather is poor by heading east via the hilltop masts and resuming the route towards Wontley Farm. A few fields later you arrive at Belas Knap, a huge Stone Age burial mound that despite excavation has remained well-preserved. You can actually enter a couple of the chambers, which does feel a bit eerie, especially when you learn that archaeologists have unearthed the bones of over 30 people from deep inside.

From the impressive barrow the Cotswold Way drops gradually down to the small town of Winchcombe. Over on the right is Sudeley Castle, once the home of Catherine Parr, although little of the original medieval building remains. In the Dark Ages Winchcombe ruled the sub-kingdom of Hwicce, and was an important power-base in 8th century Mercia. Admittedly, it is a little hard to picture this on a sunny day in August when hordes of tourists are milling around the honey-coloured buildings clutching expensive cameras and huge ice creams.

The main End to End route now leaves the Cotswold Way in order to head down to the Severn at Tewkesbury. But as an alternative you could continue along the trail for the final 17.5 miles/28km to Chipping Campden, and from there pick up the Heart of England Way through Warwickshire to rejoin the main route at Cannock Chase - see Alternative Route 2 at the end of this chapter.

Presuming you're heading directly for Tewkesbury, follow the Gloucestershire Way (and also, for a short while, the waymarked Wychavon Way) out of the village and over Langley Hill. The route crosses the Gloucestershire & Warwickshire Railway (a preserved line with steam engines) and via the hamlets of Dixton and Allenton heads west along field paths and lanes over the M5 towards the unmistakable landmark of Tewkesbury Abbey, with the equally distinctive Malvern Hills beyond. This is the final stage of the wandering but enticing 100-mile/161km Gloucestershire Way, which begins at Chepstow and links the Forest of Dean, the cathedral city of Gloucester and Stow-on-the-Wold, before returning to the banks of the River Severn. Yet another trail to pencil in for a later date!

Winchcombe TIC: tel 01242 602925. Tewkesbury TIC: tel 016842 95027

TEWKESBURY ▶ WORCESTER, 19.5 miles/31km

Tewkesbury may be a relatively small town, but it's steeped in history and well worth a nose around. Timber-framed, medieval buildings abound, but pride of place must go to the 900-year-old abbey, which is technically not a cathedral but in fact a parish church (and surely one of the largest in the country?). When the monasteries were dissolved by Henry VIII the townspeople bought the building from the King for £453, and hence the huge Norman tower, the restored vaulting, tombs and effigies, and so on, are still standing today. To the south of the abbey is the site of the Battle of Tewkesbury (1471), a decisive encounter in the Wars of the Roses when the House of York defeated their Lancastrian enemies and reaffirmed Edward IV's control of the throne.

The Severn Way runs past the handsome Abbey Mill, where the waters of the Avon were diverted by the monks to power their mill (it's now a restaurant). At the end of Severn Ham (a 'ham' is a small river island) the path joins the Severn proper, and at Mythe Bridge switches not just to the west bank but also crosses the county border, from Gloucestershire into Worcestershire. The Severn Way is billed as the longest riverside walk in Britain, stretching 210 miles/337km from its source on the slopes of Plynlimon in central Wales to Severn Beach near Bristol. The End to End route follows it for just over two days, and as you might expect this far downstream it's a fairly easy and obvious walk, the only potential problem being flooding after heavy rain when water levels can rise sharply.

The riverbank path leads to Upton upon Severn, a pleasant little town which offers plenty of waterside refreshment: The Swan (Banks's), King's Head (Whitbread), and The Plough Inn (Marstons). Particularly eye-catching is the so-called Pepperpot, a cupola-topped tower of a church that stands alone since the rest of the building was destroyed in the Civil War. It now houses the heritage centre. But although the town boasts its historical importance as a key crossing point on the River Severn the modern, single span bridge is not a particularly beautiful construction. Still, you need to use it in order to switch banks, and so follow the Severn Way upstream as it makes a couple of diversions away from the river. The first is around Cliff Wood and a 19th century mansion called Severn Bank, while the second and much longer departure skirts the village of Clifton before resuming the riverside route all the way into Worcester. Another historical landmark is passed on the far bank, by the confluence with the River Teme, where in 1651 Cromwell's victory at the Battle of Worcester finally saw off the Royalists' campaign and put Charles Stuart to flight until the monarchy's restoration in 1660.

Upton upon Severn TIC: tel 01684 594200
Worcester TIC: tel 01905 726311

WORCESTER ▶ BEWDLEY, 17.5 miles/28km

Worcester, like another ancient cathedral city Durham, looks
mightily impressive from the riverside. Launches and narrowboats chug
up and down; hundreds of swans are often to be found bobbing in the
water waiting for a feed; and through the leaves of the overhead trees you
can admire the 900-year-old Cathedral, containing King John's tomb and
medieval cloisters. From here, or via the towpath of the
Worcester & Birmingham Canal which leaves the Severn at Diglis Basin,
it's only a few minutes' walk to reach some of the city's other key
attractions: the Museum of Worcester Porcelain, where you can paint your
own plates; the City Museum and Art Gallery, including the River Severn
Gallery and Worcester Regimental displays; and the Commandery,
dating back to 1500 and for a while the headquarters of Charles II
before his show-down with Cromwell.

Switching to the west bank you gradually leave Worcester behind, and beyond
Camp House Inn (licensed by Cromwell after his nearby victory) the route
is forced inland via the villages of Grimley and Holt, with its small but attractive
castle. At the Holt Fleet pub the river is crossed once more, and the east bank
path resumed. Upstream from here it's a quiet and pleasant passage, opposite
the limes of Shrawley Wood; but soon you reach habitation once more at
Stourport-on-Severn, a town that owes its existence to the canal system.
In the mid 18th century James Brindley planned to link the Trent and the Severn
by an inland waterway, but after the people of Bewdley rebuffed his idea for its
western terminus he chose a new site further downstream where the Stour
and Severn met. The Staffordshire & Worcestershire Canal remains in use today
(connected at the other end to the Trent & Mersey Canal at Great Haywood)
and the basin is often a busy and colourful scene.

The remainder of the Way to Bewdley is quiet and uncomplicated,
with the woods of Ribbersford lining the hillside opposite. Bewdley's name
might come from the French for beautiful place, a description which remains
fairly apt (and many miles further on in your journey this claim is repeated by
the inhabitants of Beauly in Scotland). The handsome Georgian buildings that
line the riverfront mask a network of narrow, medieval streets, and are
complemented by Telford's attractive stone bridge. Bewdley Museum, and
the tourist information centre, is housed in the old Butchers' Shambles,
and recreates the lives of the local traders from centuries past.

Bewdley TIC: tel 01299 404740

BEWDLEY ▶ **KINVER EDGE**, 10.5 miles/17km

This relatively short stage links the Severn Way, via the Worcestershire Way, with the Staffordshire Way at the small sandstone ridge of Kinver Edge. If all these 'Ways' seem a bit confusing just remember that in effect they're just a series of linking paths and bridleways. There's absolutely no need to stick rigidly to them, but at the same time they do form a useful route that has been plotted with the best scenery, local amenities, etc, in mind. And a glance at the maps for the area as a whole will show that by switching to the Staffordshire Way there's a logical and steady progression northwards that is partly lost if you persevere with the River Severn, which ends up swinging north-westwards towards Shrewsbury.

Kinver Edge is a handy point to stop in terms of local services, but if you felt like pressing on then you could probably shorten the next day's mileage quite considerably. At the same time do bear in mind that south-west Staffs is largely rural and made up of small villages where accommodation is not always easy to find, so unless you have the self-sufficiency of a tent and camping gear make sure to plan ahead.

North of Bewdley there are walking routes along both banks. The west is taken up by the Worcestershire Way (more on that shortly), and the east by the ongoing Severn Way. The village of Upper Arley is less than four miles away, but the river valley begins to change character, becoming narrower and more wooded (this is the edge of the Wyre Forest). Every so often loud whistles from the steam engines on the Severn Valley Railway echo around the hills, and a trail of white smoke drifts across the treetops. The picturesque line runs 16 miles/26km from Kidderminster to Bridgnorth, and the huge, dramatic arch of Victoria Bridge below Upper Arley has been used in many films and TV programmes, including the 1978 re-make of John Buchan's classic 'The Thirty Nine Steps' featuring Robert Powell.

From Upper Arley the Severn Way continues via Telford, Shrewsbury and Welshpool to its source in mid Wales, but here the End to End Walk leaves the river and heads north-east on the Worcestershire Way. You're actually only going to walk the last 6-7 miles of this 47-mile/75km route which begins in the south of the county at the Malvern Hills, and since - like the Cotswold, Glos and Severn Ways before - its route is depicted on OS Explorer maps the need to purchase a guidebook is not paramount. It's also waymarked on the ground, so swap the sailing boat for a black pear (and leaf), the traditional symbol of Worcester that appears on its coat of arms. And in fact the Worcestershire Way leaves the Severn Way in the woods above the river a little south of Upper Arley - so continue to the village only if you need refreshment or a comfort stop. The route climbs up through Eymore Wood and hilly farmland to reach the village of Drakelow. Beyond is the wooded edge that makes up

Kingsford Country Park, culminating in the distinctive tree-flanked top of Kinver Edge where the Staffs Way takes over. From here you can appreciate the undulating, often heavily wooded countryside of north Worcs and south-west Staffs around Kinver - 'the Switzerland of the Midlands' it has even been called! But with the high-rise buildings of Stourbridge and Dudley visible only a few miles away you also become aware of how close you are to the Black Country and the West Midlands conurbation.

Now descend to the town of Kinver via some fascinating 'rock houses' that have been carved into the soft red sandstone over the centuries. The principal cave-like dwelling is known as Holy Austin Rock, and being owned by the National Trust it is open to the public for a few days each week.

Kinver TIC: tel 01384 872940

 KINVER EDGE ▶ SEISDON, 20.5 miles/33km

In total the Staffordshire Way stretches 95 miles/153km the length of the county, although you will just be walking the 60 miles/96km from its southern terminus at Kinver to the town of Rocester in the Dove valley. As with the previous few trails the route of the Staffs Way is indicated on Explorer maps, plus it's also very well waymarked on the ground by the traditional Staffordshire knot symbol. Sure, some of the less well-walked sections may get a little overgrown in the summer, but overall the route's in quite good shape and full of interest. Staffordshire's countryside may not be especially dramatic in terms of natural features but it's still full of variety: from quiet canal towpaths and heathland bridleways to stately parkland and unspoilt villages.

From Kinver the route heads north-west on paths and unmade lanes to the village of Enville, and in so doing passes in front of Enville Hall, with its turrets and romantic battlements. The building dates mainly from the 18th century, and as so often is the case is surrounded by beautiful landscaped gardens and grounds. From Enville follow paths to Lutley, then strike out abruptly eastwards across the fields by Mere Hall and make for the popular Highgate Common Country Park. Nearby is Halfpenny Green Airport, used by the RAF in World War II, but now a commercial airfield.

There are a number of criss-crossing tracks on the Common to the south of White House Lane, including several waymarked trails, but ignore these and instead continue through the woodland of Forest Covert before joining New Road past Blackhill Golf Club. At the end of the lane you can see the ridge rising before you, and the Staffs Way follows a pleasant course along the top of the escarpment, known as Abbot's Castle Hill. There are good views westwards

to the Shropshire Hills, including Wenlock Edge and Brown Clee Hill. In the
other direction is the Black Country and the West Midlands.

Unfortunately the hilltop route ends at the lane - if it continued any further it
would pass into Shropshire - and instead turns right to reach Seisdon.

 SEISDON ▶ **PENKRIDGE**, 19.5 miles / 31km

Beyond Seisdon the Staffs Way passes some disused workings, where sand
and gravel was once quarried. As evident at Kinver and Cannock Chase ahead,
the local soils are poor and thin, laid down in the glacial age (and originating
from what is known as Bunter Sandstone, from the Triassic period). Continue
via Furnace Grange, where ironworking is believed to have once taken place,
and northwards across open fields to the village of Trescott; then along farm
tracks and paths via Freehold Wood to the edge of Nurton village.

From the latest Explorer map you will see that the Staffs Way also shares
this small part of its route with the Monarch's Way, a long, long distance
trail (609 miles/981km!) that traces the route taken by Charles II during
his six-week flight after defeat at the Battle of Worcester in 1651. At this
point, in Staffordshire, the King was fleeing haphazardly northwards,
hotly pursued by Parliamentary forces under Oliver Cromwell.

He sought shelter at nearby Boscobel, Shropshire, where he was famously
hidden in an oak tree. Then, realising that the River Severn crossings were
tightly guarded to prevent escape via Wales, he headed back down through
the Midlands for the Cotswolds before reaching the south coast and
finally setting sail for France from Shoreham in Sussex.

More field paths via Cranmoor Lodge and Wrottesley Hall lead to lanes into
Oaken and then Codsall, and from here the route continues northwards across
the M54 near Gunstone Farm. Cross the tree-lined avenue that leads to the
impressive Chillington Hall, which like Enville behind and Shugborough ahead is
set in beautiful grounds; and continue ahead into Brewood (locally pronounced
'Brood'). At this handsome village, with its pleasant Georgian buildings and
striking Perpendicular church spire visible for miles around, you join
the Shropshire Union Canal and head north along its pleasant towpath as far as
Lapley Wood Farm. Here leave the canal and follow the farm drive towards
Lapley itself, an attractive village with several fine old buildings, then footpaths
via Bickford Meadows Nature Reserve to reach Mitton. Penkridge is only 3.5
miles/6km to the north, along farm tracks and quiet lanes, and despite its
modern facade and the wide main road, vestiges of the Saxon settlement are
still evident in the older parts of the village, especially around the
Church of St Michael and All Angels.

Stafford TIC: tel 01785 619136

PENKRIDGE ▶ **ABBOTS BROMLEY**, 17 miles/27km

The Staffs Way departs Penkridge via the towpath of the Staffordshire &
Worcestershire Canal, leaving at Parkgate Lock to follow field paths via the
village of Bednall and across the A34 in order to climb gently onto Cannock
Chase. The ever-efficient waymarks lead to the crest of the hill, and to what's
simply called the Glacial Boulder (a relic of the Ice Age that apparently
emanated from Scotland).

Cannock Chase, an Area of Outstanding Natural Beauty, is a distinctive plateau
of heath and woodland that offers some splendid walking, as well as being a
valuable home to wildlife, including several hundred deer (more details from the
visitor centre two miles to the south). It only covers 26 square miles/67 sq km,
and quite a lot of that is used by the Forestry Commission for timber-growing,
but as you cross the route of the Heart of England Way and descend from
the Glacial Boulder into the Sherbrook Valley you feel that here is a snatch of
some wild country at last! The popular path through the alders and
silver birches alongside the infant brook is delightful, but all too soon ends at
the Punch Bowl car park on the A513. Turn right, and after half a mile of
pavement and verge join the pleasant drive through Shugborough Estate,
and past the rare breeds farm and stately home. The present Earl of Lichfield,
the photographer chap Patrick, still lives in part of Shugborough Hall, but much
of the now National Trust-owned house and garden is open to the public
and is well worth a look around.

Leave Shugborough by the elegant Essex Bridge over the River Trent, the longest
packhorse bridge in England (14 arches), and turning right on to the towpath of
the Trent & Mersey Canal (not the river bank), follow this for 2.25 miles/4km
in the company of a new cross-county trail called 'The Way for the Millennium'.
As the unedifying prospect of Rugeley power station looms ever larger cross
over the canal and then the railway to reach the village of Colton.
Beyond is a succession of field paths and farm lanes past the southern end of
Blithfield Reservoir and into Abbots Bromley. This attractive village has a large
number of pubs, which may go some way to explaining a curious local
phenomenon that takes place every year on a Sunday in early September when
villagers adorn themselves with ancient reindeer horns and dance around the
village from dawn to dusk. And apparently they've done it every year
since the 12th century.

Stafford TIC: tel 01785 619136

ABBOTS BROMLEY ▶ ILAM, 20 miles/32km

From Abbots Bromley the route field-hops north past Bagot Forest, a remnant
of the ancient royal Needwood Forest (the old hunting rights to which probably
explains why the odd folk of Abbots Bromley still dance about each year) to
reach the pleasant market town of Uttoxeter. There is a statue of
Dr Samuel Johnson in the market place, who when young once refused to help
on his father's bookstall here - then returned as an old man to stand in the rain
as a penance. The Way leaves the town past the station and National Hunt
racecourse and crosses the wide river plain before negotiating the busy A50 via
a new underpass. Cross the old Dove Bridge and enter Derbyshire.

The next four miles to Rocester skirt the eastern rim of the lovely Dove valley,
and from the top of the escarpment you should be able to glimpse the fairy-tale
shapes of Alton Towers in the wooded hills to the north-west. Cross back into
Staffordshire at Rocester (it rhymes with 'toaster'), a small town settled since
Roman times. This is where we bid goodbye to the Staffs Way, which continues
along the Churnet Valley, and now it's the turn of the Limestone Way,
or at least parts of it, to lead you into the Peak District.

The newly-rebuilt centre of Rocester can be avoided by turning right behind
Arkwright's Tutbury Mill (built in 1781/2), and at the end of the lane beyond
St Michael's Church the Limestone Way begins its passage - look out for
the waymarks featuring a ram's head with curly horns. Once over the first
hilltop make your way briefly down to the meandering River Dove, and already
you'll notice that the landscape is palpably changing: the hills are larger and
more rounded, and the slopes are much stiffer, and as you leave the village of
Ellastone the walking steadily becomes more demanding. However, the route is
straightforward enough, staying above the wooded Ordley Brook and crossing
endless fields, then beyond the A52 it follows a gated lane almost to the hamlet
of Blore. Here the Limestone Way heads north east to Tissington, from where
you can pick up the Tissington Trail (a popular cycletrack along the course of an
old railway) and rejoin the LEJOG route at Parsley Hay. However, the main
End to End route is heading for the limestone scenery of Dove Dale, so continue
along the minor road and go over the crossroads at Blore in order to drop down
to reach Ilam, with its handy youth hostel, and into the Peak District
National Park.

Ashbourne TIC: tel 01335 343666. Ilam Hall YH: tel 01335 350212

ILAM ▶ MILLER'S DALE, 15 miles/24km

From the elegant surroundings of Ilam Park, where the youth hostel is situated
in what remains of the Victorian Gothic mansion, walk through the village and

take the roadside field path to the foot of Dovedale. Bunster Hill and
Thorpe Cloud tower above the entrance like huge sentinels. The famous,
7-mile/11km riverside route to Hartington is dramatic and beautiful - and easy -
but beware the crowds on sunny weekends. Literary associations with Dove Dale
abound, although Izaak Walton and Charles Cotton's 17th century classic
The Compleat Angler is perhaps best known. The spectacular limestone cliffs
and caves eventually give way to gentle pasture approaching Hartington, and
after the obligatory stop at one of its many cafes leave the village on the rising
lane beside the church. About two miles on take the second turning on the right
up to the A515 at Parsley Hay. Cross with care and walk the lane opposite
towards Monyash. By now you're high on the limestone plateau of the central
White Peak ('white' because of the light-coloured limestone), and in clear
weather the views are expansive and airy. The Peak National Park covers
555 sq miles (1,438 sq km), and when it was created in 1951 it was Britain's first.
Another interesting fact is that, unless you sampled some of Dartmoor a few
weeks ago, this will be the first National Park you enter on the End to End Walk
- after the small matter of 500 miles/724km.

It's worth taking a 5-minute detour down the Youlgreave turning to visit
Arbor Low, a Neolithic stone circle possibly as much as 5,000 years old.
Sometimes referred to as the 'Stonehenge of the North', the huge, surrounding
grassy banks enclose around 50 fallen stones, but the original purpose of the
enigmatic hilltop site remains a mystery.

Make sure to drop in at the Old Smithy Cafe at Monyash (a favourite of
walkers), where you join the Limestone Way once more. From the car park on
Chapel Street take to field paths north-westwards to the village of Flagg,
then deserted lanes and tracks lead to the Waterloo Inn on the A6, opposite
which a lane takes you via Priestcliffe and down to Miller's Dale.
The huge viaducts which still span the narrow gorge over the River Wye once
carried the Midland Railway's Manchester-bound steam trains, and despite talk
of one day reinstating the line for the moment it carries the altogether
more silent cycle traffic of the Monsal Trail. Ravenstor Youth Hostel is half
a mile along the road towards Tideswell.

Hartington Hall YH: tel 01298 84223. Ravenstor YH: tel 01298 871826
Bakewell TIC: tel 01629 813227

 MILLER'S DALE ▶ EDALE, 9 miles/14km

This brief stretch follows the Limestone Way until its end at Castleton,
then hops over to Edale, at the beginning of the Pennine Way.
You may appreciate a short day before the Pennines begin in earnest -
take it easy and conserve your energy. And why not allow yourself some

scenic diversions, to the top of Mam Tor, for instance; or treat yourself to something indulgent and touristy, like a tour of the show caverns at Castleton?

From Miller's Dale there are two options: the river bottom path along Monk's Dale, which is interesting for its wild flowers early on but can become awkward later, with a woodland floor of potentially slippery stones and tree roots; or a high lane above the dale's eastern rim, reached by a steep winding path via Monksdale Farm. This drops down to what has now become a grassy valley bottom track through Peter Dale and Hay Dale, eventually reaching the A623 at Mount Pleasant Farm. From here a well-walked track heads north-east across a bumpy, grassed-over area of former mineworkings, and the Limestone Way drops down through Cave Dale to end at Castleton. To your immediate left is Peak Cavern, one of four in the vicinity, and whose entrance is so high that ropes were once made and suspended in its entrance. There are guided tours to all the caverns, including a floodlit, subterranean boat journey through Speedwell Cavern.

Castleton has a large youth hostel, pubs and cafes aplenty. To reach Edale leave via Hollowford Road in the direction of Hollins Cross, a low pass and the junction of numerous tracks that flow into the Edale valley beyond. For very little extra effort you can make a short detour along the popular ridge-top path up to the panoramic summit of Mam Tor (1,200ft/365m), the so-called 'Shivering Mountain' that towers over the head of the Hope Valley. It last shivered in 1977, when part of its unstable shale hillside slid down and blocked the A625 below for good. From Hollins Cross take a good, long look at the dark massif immediately to the north: Kinder Scout. Behind you are the open and undulating dales of the southern Peak; ahead is a long stretch of high and rough upland terrain. It's wild, empty and stimulating. The Pennine miles begin here.

Descend half left for the pubs and campsites of Edale proper, or veer right for the path down to the road and Nether Booth (half mile), with the youth hostel opposite.

Castleton TIC: tel 01433 620679. Castleton YH: tel 01433 620235
Edale YH: tel 01433 670302

ALTERNATIVE ROUTE 1
BATH ▶ CROWDEN
via the Offa's Dyke Path approx 261 miles/420km

This is not a shorter route, nor is it an easier alternative to the main End to End trail. The main attraction is the splendid Offa's Dyke Path, a scenic walking route along the length of the Welsh border that is one of my favourite long distance trails of all. For the most part it's quiet and unspoilt hillcountry, but in places like the Black Mountains it can be high and remote and quite a challenge in adverse conditions. Where you leave the trail to strike eastwards for the Pennines is up to you; but the option given here is a series of linking paths across the Cheshire Plain that skirt the south east of Manchester and join the Pennine Way at Crowden.

Bath is linked to Bristol by the Avon Walkway, mostly hugging the banks of the river and passing beneath the famous suspension bridge, and from the M5 bridge there's a new Severn Way-Bristol link for walkers via Lawrence Weston and Severn Beach (see Severn Way guidebook). At Aust you join the walkway across the original Severn Bridge - a singularly peculiar walking experience - and at the far side it's a relatively short distance to Chepstow. The Offa's Dyke Path actually begins at Sedbury Cliffs on the banks of the Severn, and runs a total of 178 miles/287km to finish at Prestatyn on the North Wales coast. As a popular National Trail it's fairly well-endowed with guidebooks, waymarks, an accommodation list, and so on; but it's not a trail to be taken lightly. The Wye valley is certainly picturesque (Tintern Abbey, Monmouth, Hay) but the Black Mountains present some high and open ground along the eastern edge of the Brecon Beacons National Park. Through mid Wales the path crosses a succession of quiet but distinctly hilly valleys and ridges via Kington and Knighton, and around here King Offa's actual earthwork is most in evidence - even though we still don't really know whether it was a defence or boundary marker between Dark Age kingdoms. At Welshpool the Severn is met once more, after which you must consider where you're going to leave the Dyke: the suggested route is via the Maelor Way, which leaves at a point near Chirk; or you could carry on via Llangollen (perhaps all the way to the finish?) and strike eastwards on local paths and tracks via the likes of Chester.

The Maelor Way is a 24-mile/39km trail that links the Offa's Dyke Path at Bronygarth with the South Cheshire Way at Grindley Brook (both are way-marked, if not particularly well-walked). The 31-mile/50km South Cheshire Way ends at Mow Cop in Staffs, but just before that you can join the Cheshire Ring Canal Walk for an easy towpath walk northwards. This rather unusual trail links three separate canals and forms a continuous, 97-mile/156km circular route around the county, although you will be following just the Macclesfield Canal from near Kidsgrove via Congleton and Macclesfield as far as Marple. The remaining, short distance to Crowden can be covered in a variety of ways: study the OS Outdoor Leisure map to the Dark Peak and take your pick. The Goyt Valley Way to Tintwistle via the green surroundings of Etherow Country Park is one option, followed by a reservoir-side track along to Crowden; or perhaps local lanes to Hadfield may be quicker, from where the Longdendale Trail (part of the new Trans Pennine Trail) strides along the southern side of the valley. It may be wise to stock up before you reach Crowden, which offers little more than a youth hostel and a campsite, for as the main End to End route is rejoined the high and demanding Pennine miles begin in earnest. But at least the Offa's Dyke Path will have broken you in!

ALTERNATIVE ROUTE 2
WINCHCOMBE ▶ CANNOCK CHASE
via the Heart of England Way 80 miles/129km

In simple terms the choice, here, is which side of Birmingham do you want to go? The main End to End route (which is around 15 miles/24km longer) opts for the River Severn corridor followed by the low wooded hills and farmland of Worcestershire and Staffordshire, while this alternative keeps with the Cotswolds before heading for the gentle landscapes of Warwickshire and the green gap between Birmingham and Coventry. Although the Midlands scenery isn't exactly dramatic there is some pleasant walking around Alcester and Henley-in-Arden, and detours to Stratford and Warwick are also possible.

The last stage of the Cotswold Way from Winchcombe to Chipping Campden continues the theme from Bath: picturesque villages such as Stanway, Stanton and Broadway, and lofty hilltop viewpoints - in this case aided by Broadway Tower, an attractive folly from the top of which they say you can see 12 counties (I counted half that). The trail ends at the lovely arched market hall in Chipping Campden, an elegant former wool town, and from where the Heart of England Way takes up the reins. Its route is also depicted on the latest OS Explorer maps, although the southern terminus of this waymarked, 100-mile/161km path is actually at Bourton-on-the-Water, to the south. From Chipping Campden the route heads across the Vale of Evesham for Alcester (pronounced 'Ulster'), full of handsome Tudor and Georgian buildings and bustling tea shops, after which you make for Henley. This is 'Arden' country, a gentle landscape of low wooded ridges and traditional patchwork fields, where - in a reminder of central Cornwall and Devon - the local network of quiet country lanes may be just as direct and possibly quicker than an occasionally overgrown or ploughed-up fieldside path.

The route remains largely pastoral, crossing canals and passing through small villages, even though Coventry is only a day's walk to the east and Solihull to the west. At Kingsbury Water Park a former gravel quarry has been transformed into 30 lakes and pools that now cater for everyone from yachtsmen and anglers to ornithologists. A little further on is Lichfield, birthplace of Samuel Johnson

and home to the famous three-spired cathedral, after which you finally
encounter some rising ground that takes you on to the small but attractive
heathy upland of Cannock Chase. The Heart of England Way ends at Milford, on
the north western edge of the Chase, although the main End to End route,
entering from Penkridge to the west, heads across the heather and bracken and
drops down the Sherbrook Valley in order to reach Shugborough Hall.

the NORTH COUNTRY & BORDERS

EDALE TO EDINBURGH
329 miles/530km

EDALE TO MALHAM
77 miles/124km
MALHAM TO DUFTON
83.5 miles/134km
DUFTON TO JEDBURGH
92.5 miles/149km
JEDBURGH TO EDINBURGH
76 miles/122km

For much of this long and demanding section you will be walking probably the finest and certainly the most challenging upland trail in the UK. When the Pennine Way was opened in 1965 it was Britain's first official long distance footpath, and although it's not the longest (the South West Coast Path is nearly 600 miles/965km), nor the most popular (the albeit unofficial Coast to Coast Walk probably just pips it), its 250-mile/402km route north along the backbone of England is by turns scenic, dramatic and always full of interest: from the desolate peat bogs of the Peak District to the windswept hilltops of the Cheviots; the unique limestone landscape of the Yorkshire Dales to the historic barrier of Hadrian's Wall. And although the huge urban sprawls of Greater Manchester and West Yorkshire flank the route's early stages, the Pennine Way always keeps to the high and remote ground. Indeed, there are some stages that are entirely devoid of habitation and shelter, which means you must make sure you have adequate provisions in terms of food and drink, emergency gear, and so on, as well as the necessary competence with a map and compass. It didn't really matter if you took a wrong turning on the Somerset Levels, but getting lost on the wild and exposed upper slopes of Cross Fell (2,930ft/893m) is a different matter altogether.

The End to End route leaves the Pennine Way a few miles short of its conclusion at Kirk Yetholm to follow Dere Street, a mostly green but well-preserved Roman road, as far as Jedburgh. Here you pick up short sections of two further, waymarked trails: the St Cuthbert's Way up to Melrose, then the Southern Upland Way to near Peebles. The final stretch to Edinburgh is via local paths and lanes before a crossing of the small but lofty Pentland Hills, and the pleasant Water of Leith Walkway into the city or finishing on the outskirts at Balerno.

Inevitably there are countless guidebooks to the Pennine Way, the route of which is depicted on the succession of OS Outdoor Leisure maps that cover the length of the Pennines. You might find that maps alone will be sufficient; or perhaps a small guidebook will give you some interesting background information. What you almost certainly will want to carry is the Pennine Way Association's accommodation booklet, which gives up to date details of B&Bs and campsites. Another option is to use youth hostels the entire distance, and if this is the case you can book them all in one go and in advance using the YHA's handy Pennine Way Booking Service (but bear in mind that the location of some will alter the day stages and make the last two redundant unless you continue to Kirk Yetholm). Contact details can be found at the end of this book.

As far as alternatives are concerned, the Pennine Way is really the only option if you want to avoid the roads and built-up areas either side of the South Pennines. However, the Pennine Bridleway National Trail is currently under development, and when complete will provide a 200-mile multi-user route from Ashbourne in Derbyshire (near the end of the Abbot's Bromley-Ilam stage) to Kirkby Stephen, south of Appleby in the Eden valley.

EDALE TO MALHAM
77 miles/124km

EDALE ▶ CROWDEN
16 miles/26km
CROWDEN ▶ STANDEDGE
13 miles/21km
STANDEDGE ▶ HEBDEN BRIDGE
15 miles/24km
HEBDEN BRIDGE ▶ LOTHERSDALE
18 miles/29km
LOTHERSDALE ▶ MALHAM
15 miles/24km

▲ Youth Hostel

Malham Cove

MALHAM TO DUFTON
83.5 miles/134km

▲ *Youth Hostel*

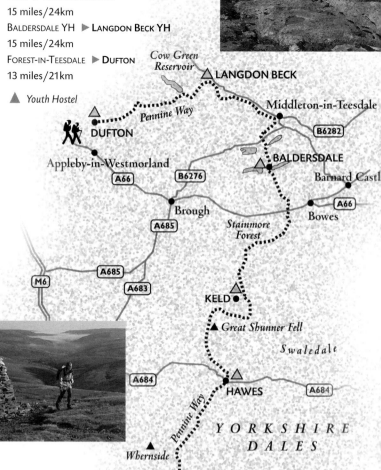

Cow Green
Reservoir
△ LANGDON BECK

Middleton-in-Teesdale
B6282

Pennine Way
△ DUFTON

Appleby-in-Westmorland
A66   B6276
△ BALDERSDALE

Barnard Castl

Brough   Bowes
A685   Stainmore   A66
              Forest

A685
M6   A683

KELD △
▲ Great Shunner Fell
                                    Swaledale
A684   △ HAWES   A684

                Y O R K S H I R E
Pennine Way   D A L E S

▲ Whernside

▲ Ingleborough   ▲ Pen-y-Ghent

HORTON IN RIBBLESDALE

                    ▽ Malham Tarn
△ Stainforth
A65   ● MALHAM
Settle   △

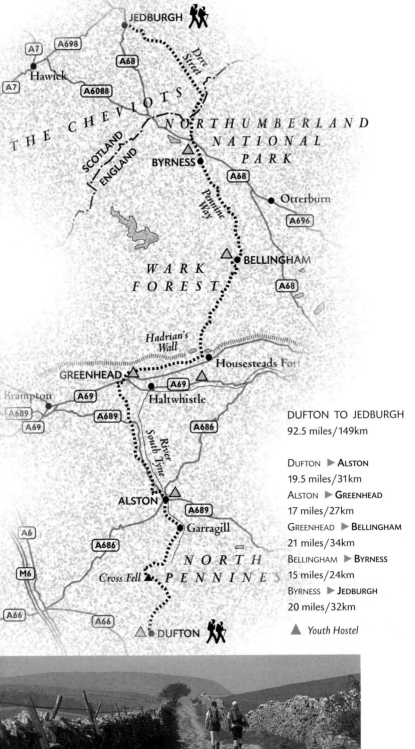

DUFTON TO JEDBURGH
92.5 miles/149km

DUFTON ► ALSTON
19.5 miles/31km
ALSTON ► GREENHEAD
17 miles/27km
GREENHEAD ► BELLINGHAM
21 miles/34km
BELLINGHAM ► BYRNESS
15 miles/24km
BYRNESS ► JEDBURGH
20 miles/32km

▲ Youth Hostel

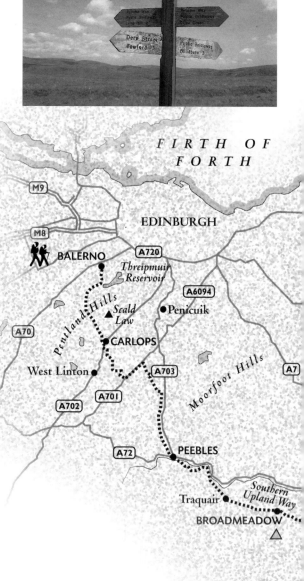

FIRTH OF FORTH

EDINBURGH

M9

M8

BALERNO

A720

Threipmuir Reservoir

A6094

Pentland Hills

A70

▲ *Scald Law*

● Penicuik

CARLOPS

West Linton ●

A703

Moorfoot Hills

A7

A702

A701

A72

PEEBLES

Southern Upland Way

Traquair ●

BROADMEADOW
△

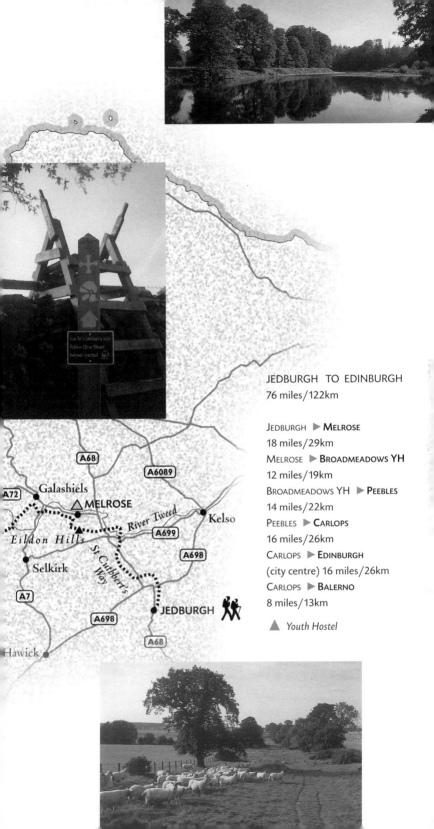

JEDBURGH TO EDINBURGH
76 miles/122km

JEDBURGH ▶ **MELROSE**
18 miles/29km
MELROSE ▶ **BROADMEADOWS YH**
12 miles/19km
BROADMEADOWS YH ▶ **PEEBLES**
14 miles/22km
PEEBLES ▶ **CARLOPS**
16 miles/26km
CARLOPS ▶ **EDINBURGH**
(city centre) 16 miles/26km
CARLOPS ▶ **BALERNO**
8 miles/13km

▲ *Youth Hostel*

Edale ▶ Crowden, 16 miles/26km

If nothing else, the End to End Walk is an ongoing geology lesson.
The previous two days have been across the broken, bleached limestone
of the White Peak, but from now on the Dark Peak offers a total contrast,
with the rougher and much higher gritstone hills of Kinder Scout,
Bleaklow and Black Hill, topped with barren moorland and blanket peat
bogs, and dotted with weirdly-shaped tors. The most eroded sections of
the trail have been laid with limestone slabs, which although it doesn't do
much aesthetically does make routefinding in the mist a lot easier.
However, always have your map and compass handy; and bear in mind that
as far as this first stage is concerned once you ascend Kinder Scout there
are no amenities whatsoever until Crowden, 15 miles/24km away.

The Pennine Way leaves the Old Nag's Head at Edale and originally headed
straight up Grindsbrook Clough behind the pub and on to Kinder Scout.
This is still a public right of way, but problems with erosion have led to a new
and rather more straightforward route: across the fields to the head of the main
valley at Upper Booth, then up on to the moors via the paved trackway of
Jacob's Ladder. This well-walked thoroughfare heads for Kinder Low, with its
trig point isolated above an eroded blanket of bog, and along the top of
the scarp to Kinder Downfall. On stormy days the wind funnels up this steep
valley head and blows the water skyward in a dramatic plume. There are distant
views of Greater Manchester, and immediately below is Kinder Reservoir and
the village of Hayfield. It was from here that the main party set off on the
celebrated Kinder Scout Mass Trespass of 1932, when working class ramblers
from the nearby cities protested for freedom of access to the private grouse
moors of the Pennines.

At Mill Hill the Pennine Way turns north-east for a long trudge along the
limestone slabs to reach the desolate Snake Pass (A57), the Glossop-Sheffield
road. The Snake Pass Inn is two miles down the road to the east.
Beyond is Bleaklow, as welcoming as its name, a high and utterly featureless
mass of moorland, marsh and cloughs (small ravines) that can make navigation
a tricky business. The route wanders up to Bleaklow Head then arcs west and
follows Torside Clough steeply down to the reservoir. Cross the Longdendale
Trail, which is part of the Trans Pennine Trail linking the Irish Sea at Southport,
near Liverpool, with the North Sea at Hornsea, near Hull; then go over the
dam and turn right to reach Crowden Youth Hostel.

Crowden YH: tel 01457 852135

CROWDEN ▶ STANDEDGE, 13 miles/21km

From Crowden the Pennine Way resumes its unrelenting upland journey north by plodding steadily up past Laddow Rocks, a popular climbing spot for over a century, and eventually out on to the bare summit of Black Hill. In dry conditions the springy, crusty peat is easy to walk across, and you can spend the time looking for mountain hares crouching in the cotton grass; but when wet it is a veritable morass, a sea of chocolate sponge pudding that slows progress and cakes itself to boots, gaiters and leggings. The actual summit trig point is called Soldier's Lump, in memory of the Royal Engineers who surveyed the hilltop in the last century, but in damp conditions it's not a spot you would wish to linger.

Black Hill, which is where you pass from Derbyshire into West Yorkshire, is the main obstacle of the day, and after this the high moorland miles across the South Pennines are relatively straightforward. A visible routefinding aid (low cloud permitting) is the Holme Moss transmitter mast, 750ft/228m high but pencil-thin, which you should keep on your right. Continue beyond the summit and then swing north to drop down to the A635 Holmfirth Road at Wessenden Head. From here the route passes a series of small reservoirs: Wessenden, Swellands, Black Moss and Redbrook, and at the A62 Marsden-Oldham road turn left to reach the facilities at Standedge.

Although it's not a particularly welcoming environment there is some birdlife to be seen on the high Pennine moors. You might have already seen, or more likely disturbed, the distinctive red grouse, which after 12th August has more than a passing walker to worry about. But over the next couple of weeks also look out for wheatear hopping from rock to rock (it has a white flash on its back), and the occasional skylark trilling unceasingly in the sky above; and if you're lucky perhaps golden plover and curlew. The latter, with its long hooked bill, is particularly distinctive, as is its drawn-out and plaintive call. Birds of prey include hen harrier, the small but speedy merlin, and in the remote crags further north perhaps a few pairs of peregrine falcon.

STANDEDGE ▶ HEBDEN BRIDGE, 15 miles/24km

Leave the hurtling A62 traffic and resume the moorland route northwards. From the high gritstone shelf of Millstone Edge (1,470 ft/448m) there are expansive views across the heavily built-up destination for much of that traffic: at your feet lies Greater Manchester, with its suburbs and motorways and international airport, and in the very far distance you might be able to pick out Liverpool and the Irish Sea.

It's inevitable that with such a population concentration either side of a high upland barrier there are going to be myriad transport crossings, and so the

Pennine Way hops across one trans-Pennine highway after the other.
The next is the Huddersfield Road, beyond which the trail crosses Rape Hill and
White Hill; then after the A672 the route takes to a slender, arched footbridge
high above the roar of the M62, a motorway not even built when the
Pennine Way was opened in 1965.

The idea for a walking route along the length of the Pennines was first
mooted by Tom Stephenson, long-time secretary of the Ramblers'
Association, as far back as 1935. Not only did it take 30 years for the
route to be officially unveiled as the first official long distance footpath
but even then the trail was incomplete, and the Scottish leg to
Kirk Yetholm was not finished until 1977. The long, drawn-out fight for
a Pennine Way was part of a wider campaign to open up the private moors
and hills of upland England to the public, and to achieve - to use
Tom Stephenson's own phrase - a 'right to roam'.

The trail continues to keep to the western escarpment of the narrow South
Pennine chain, and at Blackstone edge follows the ancient dark cobbles of what
is once believed to have been a Roman road. Beyond the A58 the path continues
past several large reservoirs, before making for the unmistakable, pointed
landmark of Stoodley Pike (Mankinholes Youth Hostel is only a mile away down
the hillside). The present tower, which replaced an earlier version that rather
alarmingly fell down, has stood since 1856 and celebrates the defeat of
Naopleon, and you can climb up to its windy viewing balcony for the views.
It's at this point that the Pennine Way is coincidental with the 50-mile/80km
Calderdale Way, which circles the busy, winding valley.
The Pennine Way now descends to the Calder where the industrial archaeology
of old mills and factories are tucked below steep wooded hillsides and narrow
wriggling lanes. Hebden Bridge, a lively and attractive former mill town that is
now home to a vibrant artistic community, is a short and easy stroll away
along the towpath of the Rochdale Canal.

Hebden Bridge TIC: tel 01422 843831.
Mankinholes YH: tel 01706 812340

 HEBDEN BRIDGE ▶ LOTHERSDALE, 18 miles/29km

This long section has its fair share of ups and downs, but generally-
speaking conditions underfoot are much easier and there's plenty
of interest along the way. Like many of your Pennine days, it begins with a
sharp upwards pull, this time out of the Calder valley and over the high
pasture via the head of the Colden valley. The American poet Sylvia Plath
is buried in the churchyard of nearby Heptonstall; her one-time husband
and former Poet Laureate Ted Hughes was born in nearby Mytholmroyd.

The Pennine Way now heads over Clough Head Hill, with airy and expansive views, before dropping back down to follow the side of Graining Water for a short distance. Further down, this watercourse merges into Hebden Water and opens up into a stunning wooded valley, the highlight of which is the National Trust-owned Hardcastle Crags. Here, among the pines, you can find the huge mounds that are home to the distinctive hairy wood ant.

The trail skirts several reservoirs before heading over the hilltop to a ruined building marked on the map as 'Withins', which is the Top Withins (or Withens) of Emily Bronte's Wuthering Heights. She once described the Pennine landscape that inspired her and her sisters as a 'distant, dreamy, dim blue chain of mountains circling every side'. Nowadays the route to Withins is signposted in Japanese as well as English. From here the Pennine Way descends to Ponden Reservoir, but if you want to visit Haworth (about three miles away) for the youth hostel and shops follow the waymarked Bronte Way from Withins. The sisters' former home at the Parsonage is now a museum, but on a busy summer's day, when the tourists throng the steep and cobbled main street of Haworth, it's hard to imagine what it must have been like for the motherless girls (none of whom reached the age of 40) in this cold and then remote Pennine village.

At Ponden Reservoir the Pennine Way passes Ponden Hall, reputedly the Thrushcross Grange of Wuthering Heights; and after this it crosses Oakworth Moor and Ickornshaw Moor, before dropping down to Cowling and Lothersdale. Paving helps on some of the boggy sections of the path, and although habitation and lanes are never too far away this can be quite a bleak and featureless land. By the end of the day the distinctive outline of Pen-y-Ghent in the Yorkshire Dales comes into view to the north, and offers a taste of what's to come.

Haworth TIC: tel 01535 642329. Haworth YH: tel 01535 642234

 Lothersdale ▶ Malham, 15 miles/24km

This is the stage where you enter the Yorkshire Dales, and the scenery starts to become less harsh and more pastoral. And it's an easy passage, too. Much of this can be gleaned from the top of Pinhaw Beacon, which is visited early on in the day, and which looks down over the Aire Gap towards Malhamdale. To the west is the distinct outline of Pendle Hill, forever associated with local legends of witchcraft, and when you reach the pleasant village of Thornton-in-Craven the circular, 45-mile/72km Pendle Way heads off into the Lancashire countryside to find out more. After a while the Pennine Way drops down to join the towpath of the Leeds & Liverpool Canal for a short distance. A reminder of the region's industrial heritage, this particular thoroughfare was 46 years in the making, and outside East Marton there's a curious double-arched bridge over the canal, where the top arch has been added to simplify the A59 crossing for today's faster and more demanding traffic. Not far on, at Williamson Bridge, the trail leaves the canal and heads for the village of Gargrave, after which it enters the Yorkshire Dales National Park.

Beyond Gargrave the route settles down to a landscape of gentle, walled pasture, of easy field paths and picturesque riverside tracks. The river in question is the Aire, which you follow via the village of Airton towards Malham, an undemanding and relaxing conclusion to the day. The dark and sometimes bleak moors of the South Pennines are now behind, and this is an altogether different section. The bright and scoured limestone scenery may be reminiscent of the White Peak of Derbyshire, but up ahead are some decidedly grown-up hills.

Malham TIC: tel 01729 830363. Malham YH: tel 01729 830321

Limestone pavements at Malham

MALHAM ▶ HORTON IN RIBBLESDALE, 14 miles/22km

For a small and fairly out of the way village Malham can seem surprisingly popular. Surprising, that is, until you walk away from the cottages and see Malham Cove and Gordale Scar for the first time. Gordale Scar is not on the route of the Pennine Way, but this deep cleft in the rock is well worth the short detour (or a visit the evening before). The Cove is a massive natural amphitheatre, whose 260ft/80m cliffs must once have boasted a stunning waterfall. The Pennine Way climbs up the western edge and out on to the fascinating, water-eroded limestone pavement that spreads across the top. The rock platform has been worn down into criss-crossing blocks, but beware the grykes (the deep fissures in between) that can trap unwary ankles. There are splendid views back to Malham and beyond; but your route continues north, over the shallow, smooth grassy valleys that are pock-marked with rock scars and sink holes (where surface water drains away).

Now for another surprise: in this area of mostly porous limestone the open expanse of Malham Tarn that suddenly appears before you is quite unexpected. In fact it sits on a saucer-shape of older and more resistant rock (Silurian Slate), and has been dammed by glacial debris. The route heads around to and through the woodland on the far side before beginning the long ascent of Fountains Fell, named after the Yorkshire Abbey that once held large tracts of land in this area. The open and exposed path requires some care in bad weather, but from the upper slopes (the route doesn't visit the actual summit as such) there are glorious views of Pen-y-Ghent, which is your next destination.

Opinions differ over the distinctive shape of Pen-y-Ghent, variously described as an upturned boat or crouching lion, almost as much as the spelling of its name. What is unquestioned is the superb panorama from its 2,277ft/694m summit, the highest point on the Pennine Way so far. The popularity of this 'Three Peaks' area (that's Pen-y-Ghent and its neighbours Whernside and Ingleborough) has led to considerable footpath erosion, and you will notice the efforts at restoration in many places. Over the years the wet and boggy stretches have been variously and not always successfully countered by a variety of means: boards, matting and crushed stone have all been deployed, but a new stone path floating on an artificial mat above the bog is proving quite effective. In several places on the Pennine Way huge limestone slabs from disused Pennine mills have been airlifted in by helicopter, but the debate over the effectiveness and validity of this approach continues.

Your destination for the day is the lonely outpost of Horton in Ribblesdale, three miles away across the bare hillside. There is accommodation locally; or Stainforth Youth Hostel is four miles down the road.

Horton TIC (Pen-y-Ghent Cafe): tel 01729 860333
Stainforth YH: tel 01729 823577

HORTON IN RIBBLESDALE ▶ **HAWES**, 14 miles/22km

This is yet another stage where there will be no shops or pubs in the miles ahead, and very little shelter should the weather turn rough, so stock up at the cafe at Horton. This well-known establishment is a mecca for walkers (tea comes in pint mugs, for instance), and it's seen its fair share of Pennine Way walkers over the years. Just across the River Ribble is the Settle-Carlisle railway line, which ploughs a wild and windswept course across the open moors via the dramatic Ribblehead Viaduct.

Your route heads back on to the hillside past numerous openings and depressions in the limestone, many of which provide entrances to pot holes and caves for which this area is renowned. Some are partly-hidden, while others like Jackdaw Hole and Calf Holes are cavernous, much beloved of subterranean explorers. The Pennine Way also shares some of its route here with the Ribble Way, a long distance footpath of 73 miles/118km that traces the Lancashire river from its mouth near Preston to its source on nearby Gayle Moor.

Much of the trail across this rough, open hillside is along undulating green lanes, some of them walled, and which are generally easy to follow and firm to walk. Their history is partly revealed at Ling Gill Bridge, beyond Birkwith Moor and Cave Hill, which is a former packhorse crossing dating back to the 16th century and which bears a plaque recording its repair in 1765 'at the charge of the whole of West Rydeing'. Beyond is Cam Fell, where for a short while the Pennine Way joins another popular northern trail. The 81-mile/130km Dales Way explores the length of Wharfedale from Ilkley, before crossing the Pennines to finish in the Lake District at Bowness-on-Windermere.
As you trot along Cam High Road you'll notice its considerable width and purposeful direction, so no surprise that its origins are Roman. It linked Bainbridge and Ribchester, and was one of a network built under the directions of Agricola as part of a campaign to subdue the troublesome Brigantes tribe - who incidentally made their final stand against the Romans on the nearby slopes of Ingleborough. By now you're at the appreciable elevation of 1,930ft/588m, after which you veer off along the edge of Dodd Fell and all the way down into the centre of Hawes, 'capital' of Wensleydale.

Hawes TIC: tel 01969 667450. Hawes YH: tel 01969 667368

 HAWES ▶ **KELD**, 12.5 miles/20km

Hawes is home to the famous Wensleydale cheese, and the Dales Countryside Museum, which considering your relatively short day ahead may be worth a visit before you leave; but after the solitude of the last 25 miles/40km this small market town might appear all the more bustling. There's a good range of shops, too, and it's sensible to take the opportunity to replenish your stores as you're faced with another couple of days with next to no amenities.

The Pennine Way crosses the River Ure by Haylands Bridge to reach the hamlet of Hardraw with its famous waterfall (there's a small fee for the privilege of admiring the 98ft/30m cascade). Steeply back on to the fells once more, and it's a long drag up to the huge, open expanse of Great Shunner Fell. Its flattish summit stands at 2,350 ft/716m, just a little higher than Pen-y-Ghent. There is a bad weather shelter if the wind and rain is whipping in; but in clear conditions the views are terrific. Nearby is the smaller lump of Little Shunner Fell, and Swaledale's rich pastures beyond, while to the west is the distinctively jagged outline of the Lake District mountains. A series of cairns marks the route eastwards and down to the hamlet of Thwaite.

If the wind has been howling on Great Shunner Fell the comparative shelter of upper Swaledale, with its field patchwork of dry stone walls and old barns, is a blessing. The narrow, lush valley swings north to Keld, and although there's a pleasant and easy riverside path the Pennine Way skirts the steep upper slopes of Kisdon Hill. It concludes at a footbridge below another secluded settlement, again with strong Norse roots. Apart from the Pennine Way, Keld is also the place where the Coast to Coast Walk passes through on its 190-mile/306km passage between the Irish Sea coast at St Bees and the North Sea shoreline at Robin Hood's Bay. Not surprisingly Keld Youth Hostel can be a busy place at the height of the season, so make sure to book ahead.

Keld YH: tel 01748 886259

 KELD ▶ BALDERSDALE YH (BLACKTON), 15 miles/24km

This stage marks another transition on your journey northwards: the softness and intimacy of the Dales will be replaced by the bolder and bleaker moors of the North Pennines, and you'll cross another important trans-Pennine route. There's also the choice of extending the stage slightly to take in the village of Bowes.

The Pennine Way leaves Keld and heads directly north on an old packhorse track across Stonesdale Moor to reach Tan Hill. The famously remote pub boasts that it is the highest in the England (1,732 ft/528m above sea level), and was originally built to serve the miners who worked the pits and quarries which still scar the surrounding landscape. On the top of Tan Hill you leave the Yorkshire Dales National Park behind, and for the next few miles the route bears north-east across Sleightholme Moor. This open and often very wet expanse of moorland can be difficult to navigate in bad weather, and if this is the case you can miss most of it out by taking the road eastwards ('Long Causeway')

and a track ('Sleightholme Moor Road') back to the main route above
Sleightholme Beck. A mile below Intake Bridge the trail divides: straight on if
you want to visit or are staying at Bowes (the 'Bowes Loop' adds an extra three
miles and rejoins the main route at Baldersdale); otherwise head off north west
to cross the River Greta, then the A66 via an underpass. This busy and
important trans-Pennine crossing follows the course of a Roman road, but in
fact the route through the so-called Stainmore Gap dates back to the tribes and
traders of prehistoric times.

The rest of the stage is across quiet and empty moorland before dropping
down into Baldersdale. The youth hostel lies between Balderhead and Blackton
Reservoirs.

Baldersdale YH: tel 01833 650629

 BALDERDALE YH (BLACKTON) ▶ LANGDON BECK YH (FOREST IN TEESDALE)
15 miles/24km

Baldersdale is a quiet and seldom-visited valley, dominated by its soul-less
reservoirs which supply the thirsty folk of Cleveland. The Pennine Way continues
northwards through walled pasture, and as the hillside rises there are new views
ahead to Lunedale and Teesdale. After dropping into the former, another small
valley given over to artificial water-collection, the route continues over the
hillside and prepares to cross the River Tees and enter Middleton-in-Teesdale.
This large and popular village now hums with walkers and tourists, but 150 years
ago it was the centre of the local leadmining industry, dominated by the
Quaker-run London Lead Mining Company. The organisation finally folded in
the early 20th century, but you can still see the miners' cottages scattered
throughout the dale. The Pennine Way doesn't actually cross the river and enter
it, but instead turns abruptly left and heads upstream along the south bank
of the Tees.

From here the final eight miles of the day are delightful, an easy and obvious
riverside walk through the wonderful scenery of upper Teesdale. Look out for
birds like dippers and grey wagtails, and in early summer admire the profusion
of wild flowers (what a contrast many miles downstream where the Tees flows
out into the North Sea via the industry of Middlesbrough and Teesside!).
Your attention will no doubt be caught by the slender Wynch Bridge,
the original version of which was built in 1704 for local miners and is claimed to
be the first suspension bridge in England. Just beyond is the pleasant waterfall
of Low Force, then a little further on is its bigger and more spectacular older
brother. High Force is where the Tees plunges over the Whin Sill (low, dark cliffs
of dolerite), and it does so in thunderous fashion. Although it's not the
highest waterfall it's certainly one of the largest in the country. Both waterfalls

are popular sites, although most of the crowds are to be found on the far bank
where the road is; but it's hard to resist stopping and staring down at the
crashing water and into the dark peaty pools. Just past Cronkley Farm the trail
switches banks, near Forest-in-Teesdale, and continues upstream as far
as Saur Hill Bridge. To reach Langdon Beck Youth Hostel turn right for a path
up to the road.

Langdon Beck YH: tel 01833 622228

 LANGDON BECK YH (FOREST IN TEESDALE) ▶ **DUFTON**, 13 miles/21km

In the big picture of things - the south-north progression of the Land's End to
John o'Groats route - the next stage might seem a trifle odd, as the
Pennine Way makes a bold move westwards before turning abruptly on its heels
at Dufton and after surmounting the considerable barrier of Cross Fell head
for Alston. It takes in some more waterfalls, high and wild moorland,
and the truly spectacular valley head of High Cup. However, if the weather is
particularly rough - and Cross Fell is the highest and probably the most exposed
spot on the whole of the Pennines - you could omit this deviation by taking
the minor road down to Cow Green Reservoir, then the well-defined track via
old mine workings as far as the B6277, and after some straightforward tarmac
miles rejoin the Pennine Way at Garrigill, south of Alston. An easier option,
but far less dramatic scenery-wise.

From Saur Hill Bridge the Pennine Way makes for Cauldron Snout,
another impressive and noisy stairway of falls and cataracts as the Tees is
squeezed between the rocks. Above is the dam for Cow Green Reservoir, the
plans for which aroused great controversy from botanists and naturalists back in
the 1960s, and today the area is a national nature reserve famous for its wild
flowers such as spring gentian. Now you enter Cumbria for the first time,
and the trail heads out across miles of open moorland via the boggy corridor of
Maize Beck. In bad weather this part requires careful navigation, although it's
generally well-walked and also defined by a string of helpful 'Keep Out'
notices provided by the Ministry of Defence, whose Warcop range lies to
the south.

And then, all of a sudden, the desolate moorland suddenly vanishes, and
at your feet is the most extraordinary scene. High Cup is a deep, narrow valley
whose smooth and perfectly rounded sides rise up into a long line of dark cliffs.
Looking down from a spot at the very back, near the fissure called High Cup
Nick, it really is the most stunning sight; and then at the far end you notice the
lush plain of the Eden valley, and if you're lucky the Lake District mountains
beyond. This small deviation of the Pennine Way is perhaps worth it after all!
After your fill of High Cup the Pennine Way drops gradually down to the

village of Dufton, where there is a youth hostel and pub; and three miles away is the larger town of Appleby.

Appleby TIC: tel 017683 51177. Dufton YH: tel 017683 51236

 DUFTON ▶ ALSTON, 19.5 miles/31km

This is a long section, involving a stretch of high and exposed hilltop, so make an early start and fingers crossed for good weather! The ascent is mainly in the first part of the day, a steep and unremitting pull up towards Knock Fell. Around you are numerous shake holes, which are small circular depressions caused by subsidence; and elsewhere in this area there are scores of disused workings, spoil heaps, and other debris left over from doomed attempts at lead mining. The map is littered with the evidence: shafts were of course the vertical tunnels that connected with levels that were dug horizontally into the veins of lead ore (or 'galena'). Another feature you'll see marked on the map is a 'hush' where the veins were near the surface and the earth and rock were simply scoured away to leave a deep groove or trench. And it's via the end of Dunfell Hush that you reach Great Dun Fell, with its small radar installation, which in turn links with Little Dunn Fell. Then, passing above the head of the River Tees, you finally reach the imposing 2,930ft/893m summit of Cross Fell, the highest point on the entire Pennine chain - and if you stick to the main End to End route and shun the ascent of Ben Nevis (or any other Scottish Munros for that matter) it will also be the highest spot on your whole LEJOG Walk.

It has to be said that Cross Fell experiences its fair share of rough weather, and that includes its very own wind. The Helm Wind (the 'Helm' or 'bar' is the name given to the bank of cloud that all too often sits on or just above the summit) periodically blows with great strength from the north-east, and has even been known to knock walkers off their feet. Until quite recently Cross Fell was known as Fiend's Fell, and it's easy to understand why local people once believed that it was the home of wild and evil spirits. The exposed summit often holds snow well into the year, and regardless of whether the Helm Wind is blowing you may be grateful for the stone shelter. Cloud permitting, the distant views stretch as far afield as the hills of Galloway in South West Scotland.

The rest of the journey is, thankfully, quite straightforward, and inevitably downwards, weaving its way north eastwards among the shafts and shake holes of Long Man Hill and Pikeman Hill and descending to the village of Garrigill. Here you can catch your breath, and there's pub refreshment and accommodation; but for more choice continue for four easy miles alongside the River South Tyne to Alston.

Alston TIC: tel 01434 381696. Alston YH: tel 01434 381509

ALSTON ▶ GREENHEAD, 17 miles/27km

At one point in the 19th century Alston was the world's biggest lead producer, and for a long time claimed it was the highest market town in England. But the next stage to Greenhead is relatively low and undemanding in terms of ups and downs, and there's little in the way of exciting panoramas - although after Cross Fell the day before that might be something of a relief; and certainly there will be more high and remote scenery as you approach the Cheviot Hills and the Scottish border in the next few days.

For the first half of the day the Pennine Way follows field paths and tracks along the valley of the River South Tyne, keeping above the west bank and visiting the grassy ramparts of Whitley Castle, a Roman fort built to defend local roads. Across the valley is the South Tynedale narrow-gauge railway, which chugs the short distance from Alston to Gilderdale along the route of the former Carlisle-Newcastle line, or at least its branch to Alston. Before being closed in the 1970s it mainly carried lead ore from local mines, and beyond Lintley Farm is an attractive five-arched viaduct. A little after Slaggyford ('slaggy' means muddy) the trail meets another and much older transport route, the dead-straight course of the Maiden Way. An unmistakable Roman road, the Maiden Way was built around AD80 and joins the Roman fort at Kirkby Thore with Carvoran near Hadrian's Wall.

Despite the generally low-level progress, Proudy Hill and Lambley Common afford some pleasant views, but after that there's some unremarkable farmland and the largely featureless tracts of moorland of Hartleyburn and Blenkinsopp Commons, then at the A69 follow the roadside with care into the village of Greenhead.

Greenhead YH: tel 016977 47401

GREENHEAD ▶ BELLINGHAM, 21 miles/34km

This stage takes in Hadrian's Wall and the edge of Wark Forest, and as well as containing a huge amount of interest it's also long and demanding physically, so you might consider either breaking it into two or extending yesterday's mileage and stopping off at Once Brewed Youth Hostel at Bardon Mill, near the Roman fort Vindolanda (roughly 6.5 miles/10km further on from Greenhead).

Leaving Greenhead it's just a short hop to enter Northumberland National Park and reach the route of Hadrian's Wall at Thirlwall Castle, a ruined building that itself is nearly 700 years old. Now it's simply a question of turning right and stepping out with the legionnaires for 10 miles/16km, although as you'll see almost immediately there are plenty of sections where nowadays there is nothing left of the Wall. Commissioned by Emperor Hadrian in AD122, it represented Rome's northern frontier for 250 years, but today you sometimes have to look for other clues: to the north is a defensive ditch which ran alongside of the Wall, and to the south is another called the Vallum which defined the military zone.

Your journey along the Wall will follow the Hadrian's Wall Path, a new National Trail that stretches just over 80 miles/129km from Bowness-on-Solway in Cumbria to Wallsend in Tyne and Wear. The waymarked route is easy to follow, and as you pull away up to the higher ground (the dark cliffs of the Whin Sill once more) the remains of the Wall become more evident. The infantry fort at Great Chesters has vanished, but a little further on is Milecastle 42, sitting high on Cawfield Crags. This is an exposed but exciting section, and as the Wall climbs up to Winshields Crags (1,132 feet/345m) there are great views south across the Pennines and north to the Cheviots - but pity the poor Roman soldiers in the bleak midwinter of northern England!

At Steel Rigg car park you can turn off for Once Brewed Youth Hostel and the National Park visitor centre. Beyond here the Wall continues its dramatic switchback along the escarpment, riding the cliffs that overlook the waters of Crag Lough. But all too soon, at Rapishaw Gap, the Pennine Way leaves the Wall and heads north. A mile further on is Housesteads, or Vercovicium, the most complete example of a Roman fort in Britain; but don't forget that Bellingham is still a long walk away.

The next few miles combine dull moorland and the conifers of Wark Forest, a stark contrast to earlier in the day and a quiet landscape far removed from the tourists strolling around Hadrian's Wall. It's not an exciting part of the trail, but once away from the woodland the undulating farmland around Warks Burn is more stimulating. Finally the path drops down over Ealingham Rigg into the valley of the River North Tyne, and to the grey little town of Bellingham (pronounced 'Bellinjum').

Once Brewed TIC: tel 01434 344396
Once Brewed YH: tel 01434 344360
Bellingham TIC: tel 01434 220616
Bellingham YH: tel 01434 220313

 BELLINGHAM ▶ BYRNESS, 15 miles/24km

Alfred Wainwright believed that the Pennine Way should end at Hadrian's Wall, and that the Cheviots were an outpost not directly connected to the main spine of the Pennines, but for the Pennine Way's true creator Tom Stephenson the lonely Cheviot Hills were his favourite walking ground. The moorland miles that lie immediately ahead are not exceptionally high or dramatic, but they are certainly bleak and sparsely populated, plus there are more blanketed slopes of conifers to end the day.

With little habitation ahead save Byrness until you reach Jedburgh, in Scotland, remember to stock up on supplies before leaving Bellingham. From here the route heads directly north across the heather moorland, open and featureless save for the occasional sheepfold or grouse (shooting) butt. Continue via Whitley Pike and Padon Hill, the latter named after Alexander Padon, a Scottish Covenanter who held open-air services at this spot, and on to Brownrigg Head, which affords good views of the huge bare slopes of the Cheviots to the north.

But bare slopes are certainly not the order of the day for the remainder of this stage, as the Pennine Way plunges into the endlessly blanketed hillsides of the 250-square mile/645 sq km Border Forest Park. You sampled some of it in Wark Forest yesterday, and now it's the turn of Redesdale Forest. The rides are generally firm and walkable, and there might be some wildlife (if you're lucky possibly goldcrests, crossbills or even the rare pine marten) but overall it's an uneventful and extremely quiet passage. It finally ends as you drop down to two settlements that vie with each other for the longest name: Blakehopeburnhaugh and Cottonshopeburnfoot. The stage ends at the village of Byrness, built by the Forestry Commission for its workers in the 1930s.

Byrness YH: tel 01830 520425

 BYRNESS ▶ JEDBURGH, 20 miles/32km

This final stage of the Pennine Way to Kirk Yetholm is 27 miles/43km long, and most of that is across the high and exposed tops of the Cheviots, which is why many walkers break the stage and head down to the lower slopes for farmhouse B&B or camping at some point.
However, the End to End route gets round the problem by leaving the Pennine Way at the border fence near the top of Blackhall Hill, and follows the grassy course of the Roman Dere Street down into Scotland for an easy walk to Jedburgh. But there may be some who want, or perhaps feel, that the Pennine Way deserves to be completed in full, in which case from Kirk Yetholm follow the waymarked St Cuthbert's Way for about 14 miles/22km until it meets Dere Street east of Jedburgh.

The Pennine Way leaves Byrness and heads straight up the forested hillside to emerge on the open hillside above, then north via Houx Hill with views over Redesdale and Catcleugh Reservoir (as artificial as the forest, of course).

To the east is the Ministry of Defence's vast Otterburn range, ringed by
'Keep Out' notices, while ahead is the border fence with Scotland.
Yes, at last, Scotland!

The trail dips eastwards to reach the low ramparts of Chew Green, once a
marching camp for the Romans. Now the Pennine Way heads north to a former
Roman signal station on Brownhart Law and briefly joins the route of Dere
Street. But two miles beyond Chew Green, approaching Blackhall Hill,
the End to End route and the Pennine Way part company. The latter heads off
north-eastwards for a long trek towards the summit of The Cheviot, but unless
you fancy the Kirk Yetholm detour go through a gate and follow the signpost
for Dere Street (Tow Ford) around Blackhall Hill and the grassy ramparts of
Woden Law, another former Roman fort - and down into Scotland.
The construction of Dere Street, which ran from the banks of the Forth, near
Edinburgh, to York, was masterminded by Governor Agricola (AD79-83) and is
still sometimes called Agricola's road. From Woden Law it drops down to cross
Kale Water and beyond are the outlines of the Romans' camp at Pennymuir.
From here signposts and waymarks (Roman helmets) indicate the route, partly
on tarmac and also along walled green lanes. At the footbridge by Cringlebank
the St Cuthbert's Way is joined, and ahead there's a choice of two quiet
lanes into Jedburgh.

Jedburgh's position near the border meant that for centuries it was
the focus of raids and skirmishes, an unwelcome pursuit known as reiving.
Today a local delicacy are Jethart Snails (brown, mint-flavoured boiled
sweets) that were supposedly introduced to the town by Napoleonic
prisoners of war.

Jedburgh TIC: tel 01835 863688

JEDBURGH ▶ MELROSE, 18 miles/29km

Although Scotland doesn't have too many recognised long
distance footpaths there are some new trails emerging, especially in
southern Scotland. From Jedburgh you'll touch on one of these -
the Borders Abbeys Way, which links the four great ruined Border abbeys
of Jedburgh, Kelso, Dryburgh and Melrose; and you'll also be following a
short part of another. The St Cuthbert's Way stretches a total of
62 miles/100km from Melrose to Holy Island, on the Northumberland
coast, and links a number of sites associated with the 7th century saint.
It's well waymarked, and shown on the latest Ordnance Survey maps,
plus its northern end is also relatively easy going, which may be a relief
after some fairly strenuous days on the Pennines.

From Jedburgh take any of the small lanes back to Dere Street and resume
your unswerving progress north-westwards. Cross the River Teviot via a new
suspension bridge (the original was washed away a year after the St Cuthbert's
Way was opened in 1997). Beyond is Harestanes Visitor Centre, worth a brief
coffee stop; then back on to the Roman Road, with the Waterloo Monument
close by on your right, and enticing views of the shapely Eildon Hills in
the far distance. A couple of miles along the green lane the trail turns off for
the hamlet of Maxton, after which is a lovely waterside section along the
looping River Tweed.

Stretching almost 100 miles/160km and issuing out into the North Sea at
Berwick, the mighty Tweed is one of the largest rivers in Britain. You may
see salmon fishermen standing up to their waists mid-stream, patiently and
endlessly casting; while upstream beyond St Boswells there is a footbridge
that allows you to switch banks and visit Dryburgh Abbey, a ruined 12th C
abbey that holds the grave of the famous local poet Sir Walter Scott.

Just beyond the Dryburgh footbridge the trail leaves the River Tweed
for Newtown St Boswells, and follows Bowden Burn to the village of Bowden.
Tracks lead down to woodland, and then the gradual and straightforward ascent
of the Eildon Hills (or, more accurately, the col between them).
It's no surprise to learn that the three prominent cones of the Eildons have a
volcanic origin, but that hasn't stopped the myth-makers: one has 13th century
wizard Michael Scott cleaving the hills into three, while another relates that the
ghost of King Arthur lies deep beneath them. Either way, the short pull up their
heather-covered slopes provide great views back along the line of Dere Street
to the Cheviots, and north to the Lammermuir and Moorfoot Hills.
Immediately below is the Tweed valley, with Galashiels in the distance and
Melrose, your destination for the day, virtually at your feet.

Melrose TIC: tel 01896 822555. Melrose YH: tel 01896 822521

MELROSE ▶ BROADMEADOWS YH, 12 miles/19km

Melrose is another pleasant Border town, and its attractions are certainly varied. Its abbey was founded in 1136, and was the first Cistercian abbey to be built in Scotland (and is also where Robert the Bruce's heart is reputedly buried). The game of 'Rugby Sevens' also originated here; while other places to visit include a teddy bear museum, and the Trimontium Exhibition which recreates daily life on the Roman frontier. It's worth lingering, not least because this is a relatively short day. However, you could combine this and the next for one long push to Peebles - without the diversion to Broadmeadows Youth Hostel it's about 24 miles/39km in total; but bear in mind that the central part over the exposed Minch Moor reaches 1,860ft/567m.

The Southern Upland Way now takes over from the St Cuthbert's Way, and this coast to coast trail is a much tougher overall proposition. You're only sampling one or two days of it, but in its entirety it stretches 213 miles/342km from Portpatrick in Galloway to Cockburnspath on the North Sea shore and crosses some high and remote ground.

For the moment the riverside passage towards Galashiels is easy. The large town is famous for its textiles, producing the well-known Tweed woollens, but the Southern Upland Way avoids entering the centre and after passing opposite Sir Walter Scott's former home of Abbotsford it crosses the A7 and swings north around Gala Hill and the edge of the town. Finally leaving the tarmac behind the route traverses the open hillside before descending to cross the Tweed once more by Yair Bridge.

The final section is short but more testing, initially climbing through plantations then turning north to reach the Three Brethren. These three tall cairns mark the spot where the lands of Selikirk Burgh, Yair and Philiphaugh meet, and from this lofty spot there are good views back to the Eildon Hills above Melrose. The high track continues north westwards, towards the summit of Broomy Law, but just before this turn left on to a path that drops down to the Yarrow valley and Broadmeadows Youth Hostel (which was opened in 1931 and was the Scottish Youth Hostel Association's first hostel).

Galashiels TIC: tel 01896 755551. Broadmeadows YH: tel 01750 76262

BROADMEADOWS YH ▶ PEEBLES, 14 miles/22km

The first part of this stage is a resumption of the Southern Upland Way, and a high and scenic drove road across the hilltops via Brown Knowe and the flanks of Minch Moor. Like the Pennine Way before it, this is another trail that offers great views and stimulating if demanding walking, but in adverse conditions it can be a bit of a slog and you'll have to keep map and compass to hand. The Minch Moor road (also spelt Minchmuir) dates back to the 13th century, and is supposed to have been used by Edward I and his army as they set out to conquer Scotland. When the valleys were considered too dangerous horses and carriages even travelled this high and difficult route. Today, despite recent felling, mass conifer plantations still cover a lot of the hillside, although it's not on the scale of the Kielder Forest of a few days ago.

The obvious track eventually dips down to meet a road at Traquair, which sadly is where you leave the trail. From here the Southern Upland Way heads south-west via the hills to reach St Mary's Loch, but the End to End route opts for a much gentler passage and an easy conclusion to the stage by following the B7062 all the way into Peebles.

Traquair boasts that it is the oldest inhabited house in Scotland, host to over 20 Scottish and English kings since it was built early in the 12th century. The Stuarts of Traquair supported Mary, Queen of Scots, some of whose relics are on display; and there's also a brewery on the site that produces Traquair Ale. Liquid refreshment is also to be had in Peebles, a pleasant little town whose name apparently derives from 'Pebyl', meaning a place where tents are pitched. Like Jedburgh and Melrose before it, Peebles suffered from the attentions of the reivers and cross-border troubles, and in 1549 the town was virtually razed to the ground by the English. Today it's a much more peaceful place, full of varied and well-stocked shops, and if you haven't done so already a stop over at Peebles gives you the opportunity to replace holed socks and other items of kit that might by now be wearing thin or giving out.

Peebles TIC: tel 01721 720138

PEEBLES ▶ CARLOPS, 16 miles/26km

Edinburgh is now only a couple of days away, but first you have to reach and cross the Pentland Hills, a narrow but angular ridge south west of the city. From Peebles there's no direct walking route over the forested Cloich Hills, so the best approach is to head northwards along the valley occupied by Eddleston Water and the A703. Just north of the town centre is a campsite at Rosetta, and beyond this is a track (indicated by a helpful Scottish Rights of Way Society signpost) that loops around Hamilton Hill to join a lane to Eddleston via Upper Kidston. At the village of Eddleston walk up the drive of Barony Castle (now occupied by the Scottish Ambulance College) but instead of going through the grand wrought-iron gateway take the surfaced lane to the right, then right again for a path through trees that hugs the perimeter hedge above the buildings. This continues through scrub above a burn, and out alongside pasture where you join a farm track, and then a long lane, to eventually emerge on the A701 near Cowdenburn. To the east there are good views of the Moorfoot Hills, while the Pentlands are now directly and invitingly ahead, but to reach them it's necessary to head left along the wide verge of the main road for a short distance before taking the lane off right at Whitmuir. By now you will have crossed a couple of disused railway lines, which would have made a very handy and off-road walking route. They mostly date from World War II when this area was used for munitions dumps. The quiet and winding lane leads to the village of Carlops, which has a pub; or a couple of miles along the road there are more facilities at West Linton.

CARLOPS ▶ EDINBURGH, (city centre) 16 miles/26km, or
CARLOPS ▶ BALERNO, 8 miles/13km

After the peace and largely rural surroundings of the last few weeks not every End to Ender will want to head into Edinburgh city centre. Of course it's an attractive and lively city, and with two youth hostels, some great buildings and parks, and stunning views from the summit of Arthur's Seat, there's s a lot to be said for taking a day or two off and seeing the sights, plus the Water of Leith Walkway provides an excellent pedestrian link right into the centre. However, if you wish to maintain the Walk's momentum then end this stage at Balerno.

The Pentland Hills are surprisingly lofty, with great views over Lothian and the Firth of Forth, and there are numerous opportunities for alternative walking routes: from West Linton there's an old drove road via Cauldstane Slap to Harperrig Reservoir; or more adventurously, from Nine Mile Burn (just along from Carlops), you can reach Balerno via the summit of Scald Law. However, the End to End route opts for the straightforward track from Carlops via North Esk Reservoir and Bore Stane, which at Listonshiels turns right to reach Red Moss nature reserve and the lane down into Balerno.

Balerno is a quiet and unassuming outpost of Edinburgh, the highlight of which are the lovely gardens of Malleny House - which houses Scotland's national collection of Bonsai trees, no less. From here you'll either forsake the city and press straight on to reach Almondell Country Park and the towpath of the Union Canal (in which case turn to the next chapter), or else join the Water of Leith Walkway by the junction of the A70.

The Water of Leith Walkway stretches a total of just over 11 miles/18km from Balerno to the docks at Leith, but from Balerno to the city centre it's only about 8 miles/13km. The route is shown on the latest OS maps, and on the ground it's signposted and generally easy to follow, since it uses the line of an old railway for much of the distance. There's an inevitable urban feel to it the closer in you get, but it's nevertheless a useful walking corridor into the heart of a major city.

Edinburgh TIC: tel 0131 473 3800. For Edinburgh Youth Hostels call SYHA central reservations: tel 08701 553255

the HIGHLANDS

EDINBURGH TO INVERNESS
217 miles/349km

EDINBURGH TO ROWARDENNAN
76.5 miles/123km
ROWARDENNAN TO FORT WILLIAM
67.5 miles/109km
FORT WILLIAM TO INVERNESS
73 miles/117km

From Scotland's capital city the End to End route now heads for some of the country's premier mountains, and what for many people will be the most spectacular scenery of the entire journey. There are numerous opportunities for Munro-bagging, including the chance to scale Britain's highest mountain, but overall the route is mostly low-level and follows two more long distance trails.

However, a glance at the map will also show that to reach the West Highland Way you first have to switch coasts - from the Firth of Forth almost to the Firth of Clyde. But the route from Edinburgh to the outskirts of Glasgow along the Union and Forth & Clyde Canals is surprisingly green and pleasant, and is currently benefiting from a multi-million pound makeover. From Loch Lomond it's trail-walking once more, as the West Highland Way threads its way through some dramatic landscapes: towering mountains and deep-sided glens, the bare wilderness of Rannoch Moor and the brooding crags of Glen Coe; and it all ends below Ben Nevis, the biggest of them all. From Fort William it's north-eastwards along the natural fault line, as the new Great Glen Way takes to the hillside above Loch Ness and leads back to the east coast for the final section to John o'Groats.

It almost goes without saying that Scotland offers endless opportunities and challenges to the End to Ender. The West Highland Way and Great Glen Way are 'safe' options in the sense that they are waymarked and well-walked, and mostly stick to the lower ground. The scenery is certainly great (providing the weather let's you see it), and there are plenty of opportunities to deviate from the route to explore other hills and glens. As the summer draws on you'll have to bear in mind the dreaded Scottish midge, and if you go into some areas you'll also have to take into account the stalking season and possible access restrictions. However, presumably you'll be quite fit and self-sufficient by now, so in terms of overall route why not consider all the other options by which to conclude your End to End odyssey? A route through the remote North West Highlands, a major backpacking journey in its own right, would be a wonderful if demanding finale. Just a thought.

Another possibility, and perhaps a more realistic alternative for the average End to Ender, is a route from Edinburgh to Inverness through the Cairngorms. It cuts out the need to swing across to the west coast, misses out the bottlenecks on the West Highland Way, and visits one of the most stunning range of mountains in Britain. Again it's mostly low-level, but offers plenty of opportunity to take a more demanding upland course - although the central Cairngorm passes are challenging enough in bad weather. A suggested route outline is given at the end of the chapter.

Buachaille Etive Mor, off the West Highland Way

Ben Lomond

ROWARDENNAN

A82

West Highland Way

Loch Lomond

DRYMEN

Stirling

M9

M8

Campsie Fells

Forth & Clyde Canal

A81 Strathblane

KILSYTH

Milton of Campsie

Milngavie

Kirkintilloch

M80

M73

GLASGOW

M8

M77

M74

EDINBURGH TO ROWARDENNAN
76.5 miles/123km

EDINBURGH ▶ **LINLITHGOW**
18/20 miles 29/32km
LINLITHGOW ▶ **KILSYTH**
20 miles/32km
KILSYTH ▶ **DRYMEN**
24.5 miles/39.5km
DRYMEN ▶ **ROWARDENNAN**
14 miles/22km

▲ *Youth Hostel*

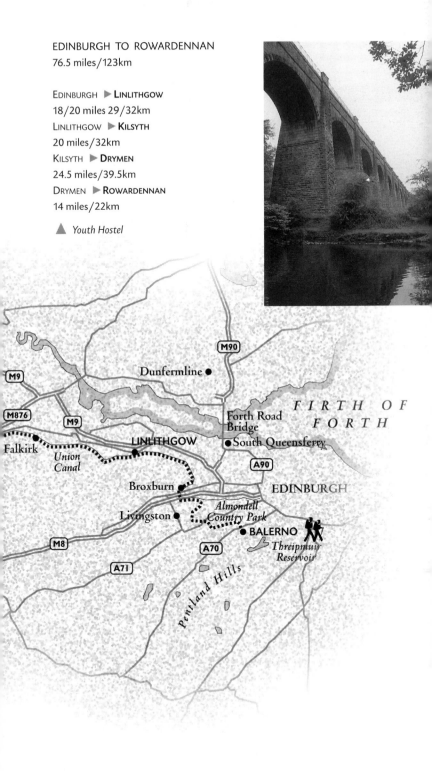

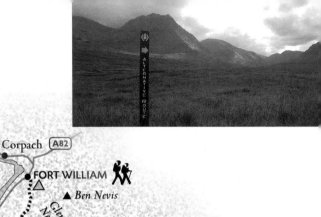

Corpach A82

FORT WILLIAM 🚶🚶

▲ Ben Nevis

Glen Nevis

Loch Linnhe

Mamore
Forest

A82

KINLOCHLEVEN

Ballachulish A82

Glen
Coe

KINGSHOUSE

▲
Buachaille
Etive Mor

Loch Ba

West
Highland
Way

R A N N O C H
M O O R

A82

Loch Tulla

Bridge of Orchy

▲ Ben Dorain

Strath
Fillan

A85 TYNDRUM

▲
Ben
Lui

Crianlarich A85

Glen
Falloch

▲
Ben
More

West
Highland
Way

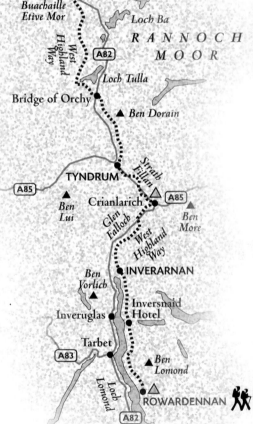

INVERARNAN

Ben
Vorlich
▲

Inversnaid
Hotel

Inveruglas

Tarbet

A83

▲ Ben
Lomond

Loch
Lomond

A82 ROWARDENNAN 🚶🚶

ROWARDENNAN TO FORT WILLIAM
67.5 miles/109km

ROWARDENNAN ► **INVERARNAN**
14 miles/22km
INVERARNAN ► **TYNDRUM**
12 miles/19km
TYNDRUM ► **KINGSHOUSE**
18.5 miles/30km
KINGSHOUSE ► **KINLOCHLEVEN**
9 miles/14km
KINLOCHLEVEN ► **FORT WILLIAM**
14 miles/22km

▲ *Youth Hostel*

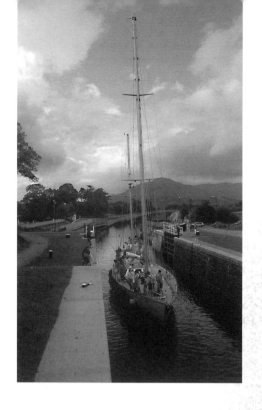

FORT WILLIAM TO INVERNESS
73 miles/117km

FORT WILLIAM ▶ **LAGGAN**
21 miles/34km
LAGGAN ▶ **INVERMORISTON**
19 miles/30km
INVERMORISTON ▶ **DRUMNADROCHIT**
14 miles/22km
DRUMNADROCHIT ▶ **INVERNESS/BEAULY**
19/14 miles, 30/22km

▲ *Youth Hostel*

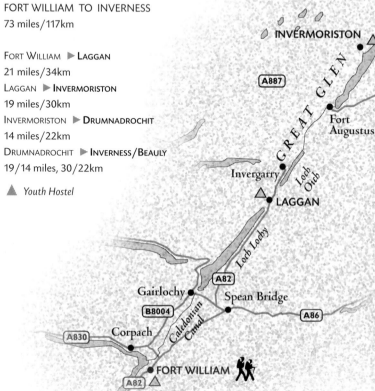

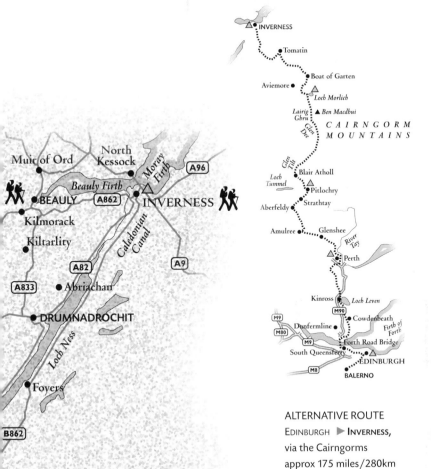

ALTERNATIVE ROUTE
EDINBURGH ▶ INVERNESS,
via the Cairngorms
approx 175 miles/280km

EDINBURGH ▶ LINLITHGOW
from city centre via Queensferry 20 miles/32km;
from Balerno 18 miles/29km

From the city centre: There are several options to re-start the walk from
the middle of Edinburgh. First, you can return on the Water of Leith Walkway
to Balerno; second, you can follow the Union Canal out of the city (a route that
should become clearer as the canal is steadily renovated); or the third way is to
head towards the banks of the Forth at Queensferry, then join the
Union Canal north of Broxburn.

The new OS Explorer map for Edinburgh shows a cycle route from the city
centre to the Forth Road Bridge at Queensferry. It's part of the National Cycle
Network, and uses a combination of minor roads, shared-use pavements
and railway paths that although mostly surfaced still provides a useful
pedestrian route out of Edinburgh. After admiring the Forth bridges you can
thread your way along the shore past Hopetoun House to join the Union Canal
near the M8 motorway.

From Balerno: With few off-road footpaths in this area the End to End route
follows the National Cycle Network Route 75 indicated on the latest OS maps
from Balerno as far as Almondell Country Park. For most of the way this is along
minor roads and lanes, and although there's not much of immediate interest
there are some better, distant views across West Lothian from the ridge
around Kirknewton.

Near East Calder you enter the green and relaxing surroundings of Almondell
and Calder Wood Country Park, which stretches for 1.5 miles along the banks of
the River Almond. The wooded drive leads down to the water, and across
the grand Nasmyth Bridge is the visitor centre and snack bar. Re-cross the
Almond by a narrow suspension bridge, and from here a path traces the route
of a canal feeder above the river's leafy east bank that eventually leads to the
high and imposing aqueduct that carries the Union Canal across the valley.
Join the towpath on the far side (you first have to go under) for a long
and level walk all the way to the edge of Glasgow.

The waterway connection between Scotland's two largest cities involves
the Union Canal from Edinburgh to Falkirk, then the Forth & Clyde
Canal from Falkirk to Glasgow. At the time of writing the route is
undergoing a huge facelift, as an ambitious project called the Millennium
Link is aiming to totally regenerate the two canals. In total it's costing
over £78 million, and new bridges are being built, locks renovated and
banks realigned, so that eventually the plan is to make the route wholly
navigable once more. However, this will also benefit the walker, as
overgrown towpaths are cleared, steps and surfaces rebuilt, and all-round
access improved.

You'll notice the effect of the Millennium Link almost immediately, as the towpath enters a newly-built tunnel below the M8 motorway (the building of which had effectively severed the canal and so blocked the walking route). There's plenty to see along the way, from the occasional overhead planes making their descent to Edinburgh Airport to the bizarre sight of the shale bings near Winchburgh (these are huge mounds of waste shale left by Scotland's first oil industry that occurred here about 100 years ago). But approaching Linlithgow the surroundings are increasingly rural, and the tree-lined route supports a surprising abundance of wildlife.

Linlithgow TIC: tel 01506 844600

 LINLITHGOW ▶ KILSYTH, 20 miles/32km

The excellent Canal Museum at the Manse Road Basin in Linlithgow tells the story of the Union Canal, as well as offering boat trips and a handy tea room. The canal is 31.5 miles/51km long and deliberately follows the 240ft/73m contour throughout, as well as maintaining virtually the same width and depth (it was nicknamed the Mathematical River). It opened in 1822 and for a short time proved very popular, but only 20 years later the arrival of the railway cut the travelling time between Glasgow and Edinburgh from over 12 hours to under three. Linlithgow is a fascinating town with a rich history, most notable for its Palace where James V and Mary, Queen of Scots, were both born.

The towpath continues westwards, crossing the River Avon by another mighty aqueduct. This elegant, 12-arched structure is nearly 900ft/273m long (second only to Telford's Pont-y-Cysyllte Aqueduct, in Wales, in terms of length), and spans the river above Muiravonside Country Park like a colossus. After this the canal heads for Falkirk, via a tunnel under Callendar Park since the estate owner at the time of construction would not allow the canal in sight of Callendar House, and ends just west of the town centre. Originally there was a series of 11 locks that took boats down the 110ft/33m drop to link with the Forth & Clyde Canal, but they disappeared a long time ago as modern Falkirk grew. However, as part of the Millennium Link there are as yet unconfirmed plans to build a brand new structure to once more convey boats between the two canals, the latest suggestion involving a huge, state-of-the-art wheel to lift whole boats! Another new construction is a lifting bridge at nearby Bonnybridge, where a section of the road will be raised into the air to allow boats to pass underneath. So keep your eyes peeled - you never know what you might see.

The centre of Falkirk is modern and busy, although the town has a place in the history books for its battles (William Wallace's army was soundly defeated in 1298, but Bonnie Prince Charlie won the day in 1746) and its Tryst, which was where drovers from all over Scotland and northern England met each year to sell their animals.

Between Falkirk and Kilsyth the canal runs loosely parallel with the Antonine Wall, which after Hadrian's Wall and Dere Street is a welcome return to things Roman. This particular construction is 37 miles/60 km long and was built in AD142 to reflect Rome's short-lived push north. The wall, which was named after Emperor Antoninus Pius, was made of stone and turf and stood about 11ft/3.5m high. Unfortunately it has not survived too well, but every now and again there are the grassy remains of forts (you can inspect two of the most prominent at Croy Hill and Bar Hill near Kilsyth) and the large ditch that was dug in front of the wall as an extra defence.

Falkirk TIC: tel 01324 620244

 KILSYTH ▶ DRYMEN, 24.5 miles/39.5km

At 35 miles/56km long, the Forth & Clyde is similar in length to the Union but in every other way is a much different prospect.
It has 40 locks and was built to accommodate sea-going vessels, since it was designed to link Scotland's east and west coasts. It opened in 1790 after taking 22 years to complete, partly because funds ran out half way through construction, and was finally closed in 1963. Now as a result of the Millennium Link it is having new life breathed into it, and it's not just the human users who will benefit. The section around Kilsyth in particular is quite rural and peaceful, and the natural environment afforded by the canal is being monitored and hopefully enhanced by the work of the project's full-time ecologist who has already advised on bat roosts under bridges and the effects of dredging on water plants.

Beyond the rooftops of Kilsyth are the Kilsyth Hills, which are in effect part of the large Campsie Fells. The proper mountains are not far away now, and in anticipation the End to End route leaves the Forth & Clyde Canal at Kirkintilloch, still a few miles from Glasgow's outer edge, to head north-east towards Loch Lomond. However, the waterway continues into and through Glasgow city centre before finally reaching the River Clyde downstream from the Erskine Bridge near Old Kilpatrick, and if you wanted to enjoy some further towpath miles you could continue as far as the lock flight at Maryhill from where the Kelvin Walkway provides a direct walking link north to Milngavie, where the West Highland Way officially begins.

Back at Kirkintlloch you join another former transport route that has also been put to good use. The Gartness-Kirkintilloch Railway may be no more, but its

trackbed has been turned into a handy off-road walking and cycling route,
and extends almost 8 miles/13km from Kirkintilloch via Milton of Campsie and
Lennoxtown to Strathblane. It's a terrific link between the canal and the West
Highland Way (well, almost), and cuts out the need to negotiate the suburbs of
Glasgow. A lane running south from Strathblane comes out opposite an
entrance to Mugdock Country Park, and after a stroll through the grounds of
the ruined castle, and possibly a cuppa at the visitor centre near Gallow Hill,
pick up the West Highland Way that runs along the southern edge of Mugdock
Wood. From here the trail runs via Craigallian Loch and over some open hillside
before joining the route of the former railway once more for a steady
northwards progress along Strath Blane. Finally the line comes to an end near
the hamlet of Gartness, where you pick up the lane east into Drymen.

Drymen TIC: tel 01360 660068

 DRYMEN ▶ ROWARDENNAN, 14 miles/22km

The West Highland Way was opened in 1980 as Scotland's first official
long distance trail. It runs for 95 miles/153km from Milngavie, three
miles south of Mugdock, to Fort William, and passes through some
outstanding scenery. The route is waymarked, documented in guidebooks
and shown on maps, plus it is very well used. Although there are B&Bs,
campsites and a few youth hostels along the way there are some long
stretches which are quite wild and devoid of any facilities, so as on the
Pennine Way make sure you stock up beforehand. The sight once again of
other, backpacked walkers may come as something of a surprise, but it's
likely you will have travelled just a little further than most of them!

Although the hills have been impinging for a couple of days now it's not until
after Drymen, when you enter the Queen Elizabeth Forest Park, that the
Highlands start in earnest. Walking the WHW for the first time, nearly 20 years
ago, I found the first day from Milngavie something of a disappointment, but on
the second day it really took off. From Drymen the first few miles through
Haradhban Forest are rather routine, but then you emerge on high open hillside
and from the upper slopes of the aptly-name but relatively modest Conic Hill
(1,184ft/361m) there are terrific views over Loch Lomond. To the north
the huge expanse of water is ringed by such massive peaks as Ben Vorlich and
Ben Lomond, while in clear weather the view the other way stretches beyond
Glasgow and the Firth of Clyde to the peaks on the Isle of Arran.

The route drops down to Balmaha, with its handy tearooms, and from here
it's a question of following the eastern edge of the loch northwards for almost
20 miles/32km along a combination of waterside paths, woodland tracks and
a stretch of surfaced road. Covering over 27 sq miles/70 sq km, Loch Lomond is

Britain's largest stretch of inland water and has 38 named islands known as inches (from the Gaelic 'innis'). One of these is Inchmurrin, named after St Mirrin who founded an early Christian settlement on the island; but in more recent times was also home to a naturist colony known to local people as the Danglers. The whole of Loch Lomond, together with the nearby Trossachs, is set to become Scotland's first official National Park, and at Rowardennan a new National Park centre is being built with special walkers' facilities (including boot wash and rucksack lockers).

Rowardennan Youth Hostel is the usual stopping point mid way along the eastern shore of Loch Lomond (there's also a campsite), and in summer a passenger ferry connects with the small settlement at Inverbeg on the opposite shore. Finally, if you really felt energetic or masochistic and wanted to polish off a few Munros during your walk you could always take time out here to ascend the 3,196ft/974m of Ben Lomond, the most southerly of the Munros and whose popular summit path starts nearby.

Rowardennan YH: tel 01360 870259

Rowardennan ▶ **Inverarnan**, 14 miles/22km

Not a long stage in terms of distance, but potentially tricky underfoot, since the shoreline gets rougher and more difficult as you move further along the fjord-like northern arm of Loch Lomond. It's also quite isolated, other WHW walkers notwithstanding, as the main road and railway hog the loch's opposite, western shoreline throughout.

To start with there is the choice of rough, wooded shoreline path or higher forest ride along the lower slopes of Ben Lomond. The former passes Rob Roy's Prison, a small rock cave by a large crag where the legendary Scottish outlaw supposedly kept his hostages. Loch Lomond and the surrounding high ground was Rob Roy MacGregor's territory, although he only took to the hills after his droving business failed and he was bankrupted by the Duke of Montrose. He got his own back, of course, by stealing the Duke's cattle and kidnapping his men. Ironically, despite his antics (and the romanticised sheen put on them by Sir Walter Scott's novel) Rob Roy's life ended quite peacefully, dying in bed aged 63.

As the two routes merge the views across the loch remain impressive, with the craggy outline of the Arrochar Alps prominent. At Inversnaid there is a hotel at the head of the small road from Loch Katrine, but westwards there's only the ferry across to Inveruglas. The remaining six miles of the lochside are still mostly wooded, but underfoot the boulders and broken rock can be a little tricky in wet weather. Not insurmountable, just slow-going. A short distance from Inversnaid is a well-visited cave that once again is associated with Rob Roy, and before that with Robert the Bruce. The word 'CAVE' is helpfully painted in vulgar white letters on the rock should you have any difficulty locating it.

Gradually the forest thins out for clearer views of the mountain wall dominating the head of Loch Lomond, including Ben Oss and Ben Lui. The trail continues beyond the end of the loch into Glen Falloch, and at Beinglas Farm (where there is a handy campsite) you can turn left to reach the old cattle drovers' inn at Inverarnan - from here they used to make for Crieff or Falkirk, which you walked through only a few days ago. Accommodation and refreshment is also available at Ardlui, 1.9 miles/3km south along the main road; or else you could continue along the WHW for a further 6.5 miles/10km for more facilities including a youth hostel at Crianlarich.

Crianlarich YH: tel 01838 300260

INVERARNAN ▶ TYNDRUM, 12 miles/19km

The next stage begins with a relatively easy plod along the floor of Glen Falloch, past a few surviving remnants of the old Caledonian pine forest. Most of the route is along the line of an 18th century military road, and this will become a familiar feature over the next few days. In the early 1700s the threat of repeated Jacobite insurgency forced the English to review their military operations in the Highlands. To aid future strategy they embarked on a detailed mapping exercise (and hence the Ordnance Survey was born), plus they gradually introduced a systematic and reliable road system in the Highlands to enable troops to move swiftly and effectively. Under General Wade (and later Major Caulfeild) a network spread into the Scottish hills, and although quite a few have since been replaced with modern highways many of these well-made routes are still evident today. One of the original roads from the Central Lowlands all the way to Fort William is now the basis for long chunks of the West Highland Way north of Loch Lomond.

The Way doesn't actually enter Crianlarich, partly because there's not much there (it grew up around the railway), and also because while high in the trees above the settlement the trail turns abruptly north west to join Strath Fillan. From the viewpoint there is the great sight of the giant pyramidal shape of Ben More, directly ahead, but once again the route adopts a low-level course as it descends through the forest to cross the railway, road and river to reach the remains of St Fillan's Priory. St Fillan was an 8th century Irish monk who wandered around the Highlands preaching Christianity.

The Way follows the bank of the River Fillan before entering plantations, as it does so it passes a site known as Dal Righ. It means the King's field, and is believed to be where Robert the Bruce was defeated by the MacDougalls of Lorne in 1306. Beyond the trees is Tyndrum, and a welcome chance to stock up on supplies, especially since the next shops you'll meet will be two days away at Kinlochleven.

In fact tourism is the only thing that keeps Tyndrum going, as the coaches and cars pulling into the souvenir shops will testify. However, the row of cottages you pass at the adjoining village of Clifton are a reminder that this settlement was once the scene of a small but busy lead-mining industry in the late 1700s. Another curious feature for somewhere so small and remote is that Tyndrum, like Crianlarich originally, has the distinction of having two railway stations, since it was served by two separate lines built by rival companies (the Caledonian and North British) who were evidently not in the business of co-operation!

Tyndrum TIC: tel 01838 400246

TYNDRUM ▶ KINGSHOUSE, 18.5 miles/30km

To many people the crossing of Rannoch Moor to reach Kingshouse and Glen Coe is the highlight of the WHW. Wild open moorland surrounded by breathtaking mountain scenery, the essence of the Highlands. The trail itself is not particularly arduous in terms of terrain, since much of the route sticks to the reliable old military road, but for nearly ten miles it is utterly open and exposed, and in really bad weather you could consider breaking the stage at Bridge of Orchy or Inveroran.

From Tyndrum you now head directly north in the company of the road and railway which both squeeze along the bottom of upper Glen Orchy, and at one point the railway does a wonderful loop around the lower part of Auch Gleann to maintain height. The views are dominated by more huge mountains, this time the rocky bulk of Beinn Dorain (3,530ft/1,076m) which looms overhead and rather appropriately means hill of the scorching. Bridge of Orchy is another small and isolated outpost, and the hotel offers a welcome bunkhouse for walkers.

By now you will have got used to the old military road: a consistent width and usually firm underfoot, and carefully engineered so that it uses the slopes. The track now snakes its way up the low hillside above Loch Tulla, from where there are the first proper views of Rannoch Moor, and a chance to appreciate its desolation and vastness. On the far side of hill is the hotel at Inveroran, which is the last chance of shelter before the lonely 9.5 mile/15km walk to Kingshouse along the western edge of Rannoch Moor. There's been an inn or hotel on this site for over 200 years, and during that time it's played host to a variety of customers, from drovers with their large herds of cattle and flocks of sheep, to many of the early Scottish mountaineers who pioneered the first winter routes on the surrounding peaks.

The military road leaves the shelter of the pines behind and heads out across the open slopes of Black Mount. The rivers, lochans and bogs of Rannoch Moor stretch out endlessly to the east, ringed by a line of hills and mountains; and apart from Ba Bridge and some tiny pockets of conifers the views are all of space and distance. Finally, with the road to Glen Coe drawing near, the posts and cables of the White Corries Ski Centre appear on the left, leading up to the craggy tops of Meall a' Bhuiridh. At Blackrock Cottage the WHW joins its approach road and drops down to the Kingshouse Hotel.

KINGSHOUSE ▶ KINLOCHLEVEN, 9 miles/14km

This short stage, which includes just one sharp climb at the very beginning, reflects the fact that as far as B&B accommodation is concerned

Kinlochleven is the only realistic option between here and the end of the trail at Fort William. Obviously if you carry a tent and stove you can be more flexible, or perhaps even make the Fort in a day if the weather is good and you feel fit. And if you don't feel fit by now, 950 miles/1,530km on from Land's End, then perhaps you never will!

There is surely no grander nor isolated place to stay on a British walking trail than at Kingshouse. The hotel sits entirely alone at the far corner of Rannoch Moor and is surrounded by some of the most majestic mountains of the Highlands, chief among which is Buachaille Etive Mor, or the Great Herdsman of Etive. South of this is the wild corridor of Glen Etive, while to the west is the forbidding barrier containing the Pass of Glen Coe. The WHW exits northwards, as the so-called Devil's Staircase winds its way up the hillside above the A82 in a series of zig-zags for about 850ft/260m. Bearing in mind that this is still the old military road it must have represented quite a feat of construction given the date (around 1750) and the primtive tools that the soldiers had to work with then. But, despite the chatter in the bar of the Kingshouse the evening before, the Devil's Staircase is not half as bad as it's made out to be. From the top there are impressive views back towards the Pass, and new vistas in front including the angular tops and ridges of the Mamores and, for the first time, the mighty shoulder of Ben Nevis looming in the background.

From here it's an open but relatively straightforward walk across and then down to Kinlochmore and Kinlochleven, at the eastern end of Loch Leven. As you descend through patchy woodland the last mile or so is alongside the huge pipes that run down the hillside from Blackwater Reservoir, purposefully built a century ago to feed the aluminium smelter at Kinlochleven. The modern town grew up to serve the works, and as such is a functional rather than a pretty kind of place.

 KINLOCHLEVEN ▶ FORT WILLIAM, 14 miles/22km

The final stage of the West Highland Way begins along the B863 out of Kinlochleven, a road which was considerably busier before the bridge across the mouth of Loch Leven was built at Ballachulish in 1975. There are good views down the sea loch to the Pap of Glencoe (Sgorr na Ciche) as the Way climbs the hillside, quite steeply in places, then from the top new views of the Mamore Hills are revealed. The route now heads westwards along the bottom of a wild and unspoilt glen via Lairigmor, and once more it's the trusty old military road. Eventually it swings north and climbs through woodland, and near the isolated outpost of Blar a Chaorainn the old road turns becomes modern and surfaced and leads northwards down to Fort William. However, the trail veers away north-eastwards, drawn like a magnet towards Ben Nevis, and as it plunges down through forested hillside towards Glen Nevis there are new views of the mountain, awesome in its sheer size.

The twisting track through Nevis Forest visits Dun Deardail, an Iron Age hillfort described as vitrified because the rock defences became fused after being subjected to prolonged, intense heat (they were probably encased with timber originally). The track eventually reaches the valley floor to emerge near the modern visitor centre, and the beginning of the popular summit path for Ben Nevis. Back along Glen Nevis is the youth hostel and campsite; ahead is the lane to Fort William, Loch Linnhe and the Great Glen.

Newly surveyed, the height of Ben Nevis is now given at 4,409ft/1,344m. Either way, it remains the highest mountain in Britain; and since you're connecting the two most extreme ends of the country on foot why shouldn't you bag the highest point while you're at it? It almost seems churlish to ignore the opportunity! However, it's not something you can polish off after supper. You'll need to set aside a day to 'enjoy' it properly, and much will depend on the prevailing weather, since the upper slopes of the Ben often spends a good part of its time wreathed in cloud. The main route to the summit is about 12.5 miles/20km for the round trip (usually around 5-6 hours of walking) and follows a bridleway established in 1883 to serve the weather observatory. It's a steady climb, but not particularly difficult, and although the actual summit gives very little impression of the mountain's sheer height and size (especially its rugged north face) the chance to add yet another noteworthy highlight to the trip is surely irresistible?

Fort William TIC: tel 01397 703781. Glen Nevis YH: tel 01397 702336

Rannoch Moor - following page

FORT WILLIAM ▶ LAGGAN, 21 miles/34km

Although many visitors to Fort William will do little more than gaze
up at Ben Nevis in awe, a fair number are there to walk, climb, ski, etc,
and the facilities reflect this - from the well-stocked outdoor shops to the
independent backpackers' hostel. Maybe as a result of this Fort William
always seems busy, with something of a frontier spirit as people get ready
to depart for somewhere else. It not only acts as a gateway to
the mountains, but also to the West Coast islands via Mallaig and Oban;
and sitting on a sea loch at the western end of the Great Glen, that
dramatic geological fault line that rips through the centre of upland
Scotland, it's part of the link between the Atlantic and the North Seas.

If you're planning to reach John o'Groats via the North West Highlands this may
well be the point at which you depart the main route, since the End to End now
switches direction and aims for the east coast. To do this it uses the new Great
Glen Way, the last proper long distance footpath of the entire journey. The only
problem is that at the time of writing the trail is still under construction.

When I undertook my first End to End research in the early 1990s I completed
the Fort William-Inverness stage using the Great Glen Cycle Route, a pleasant
and mostly off-road route combining canal towpath and rough hillside tracks
through Forestry Commission plantations above Lochs Lochy and Ness.
Great for cyclists and walkers alike, of course. But work has finally begun on
the long-awaited Great Glen Way, the fourth official long distance footpath in
Scotland (the West Highland Way, Southern Upland Way and Speyside Way are
the others). It's due to open in summer 2002, will stretch for 73 miles/117km
between Fort William and Inverness, and of course will be waymarked and
accompanied by an official guidebook. The new trail will share some sections
with the Cycle Route, but elsewhere negotiations are continuing with
landowners to create totally new stages - so the exact directions and distances
are for the moment approximate, and by necessity some of the following
description is rather vague.

The Great Glen, also known as Glen More or Glen Albyn, is a long and narrow
corridor running sharply north-eastwards, the finest example of a tear-fault in
Britain and still the most active earthquake zone in the country. It was inevitable
that the Great Glen Cycle Route and the impending Great Glen Way would end
up sharing some of their routes. The latter is due to start at the site of the
old fort, which rather unromantically is on a piece of land near Safeways
supermarket, and in future years this may also be where the West Highland Way
officially links up with it. However, for much of its early stages both the footpath
and the cycle route run together along the towpath of the Caledonian Canal,
which heads east from a flight of locks known as Neptune's Staircase to
Gairlochy. If the cloud-base is not too low there should be stunning views of

Ben Nevis and Aonach Mor from this point. At Gairlochy the canal
issues out into Loch Lochy, and the walking/cycling route heads along the
northern shore, first of all along a quiet lane and then on a long series of forest
rides not far above the waterside. Loch Lochy Youth Hostel is off the main road
at South Laggan.

Fort Augustus TIC: tel 01320 366367
Loch Lochy YH: tel 01809 501239

 LAGGAN ▶ INVERMORISTON, 19 miles/30km

Another longish stage, but like the previous one it's relatively straightforward,
involving lochside tracks and canal towpaths. It begins at Laggan where the
Great Glen Way continues beyond the Water Park (a small chalet development)
and follows the route of an old railway along the southern side of Loch Oich
to Aberchalder; then it's the Caledonian Canal towpath once more to reach
Fort Augustus where the waterway descends by a series of five locks to
enter Loch Ness.

The Caledonian Canal was built in the early 19th century by
Thomas Telford, that most famous of Scottish engineers, and its story is
told in the excellent Canal Heritage Centre beside the locks at Fort
Augustus. Comprising ten swing bridges, two aqueducts and 42 pairs of
lock gates, the Canal was much more expensive than first planned and its
18-year construction was considerably longer than envisaged. However, it
finally eliminated the need for the treacherous north coast journey around
Cape Wrath and through the dangerous Pentland Firth, and it's a
remarkable sight to see large, ocean-going yachts and deep-sea trawlers
motoring past you as you stroll along the towpath (quite a difference to
the horse-drawn barges way back on the Grand Western Canal in Devon!).
In recent years many of the locks and bridges have been refurbished,
and nowhere does the Canal look so neat and attractive than at the locks at
Fort Augustus. The small settlement here was originally known as
Kilchumein, but was renamed in honour of William Augustus,
Duke of Cumberland, who vanquished Bonnie Prince Charlie at Culloden
in 1746. Although the original forts (first wooden, then later stone) of
the Great Glen have now disappeared, they once formed a line of military
strongholds built by the English to subdue the Clans after the first
Jacobite Rebellion in 1715. Fort William, for instance, was named after
King William III and around 600 troops were housed in its barracks.

Beyond Fort Augustus both the walking and cycling routes take to
the northern shore of Loch Ness, and follow rough tracks through Forestry
Commission land high up on the hillside above the water to Invermoriston.

The Grants of Invermoriston offered shelter to the fleeing Prince Charles after Culloden, and Johnson and Boswell stayed at the former Invermoriston Inn while planning their tour of the Hebrides. Today there is simple B&B on offer, and camping along the road to the south. Loch Ness Youth Hostel is a further four miles at Alltsigh, on the lochside beside the A82, but if your legs are still strong it's advisable not to use the busy and narrow main road but continue along the hilly forest track to reach the building.

Fort Augustus TIC: tel 01320 366367. Loch Ness YH: tel 01320 351274

 INVERMORISTON ▶ **DRUMNADROCHIT**, 14 miles/22km

The forest rides continue well above the lochside and provide glorious, sweeping views over Loch Ness. Closer to hand look out for red squirrels, and among the more traditional pines crossbills and crested tits may be spotted. Although there are occasional waymarks the route is obvious, and for the most part is also wide enough to cater for walkers and cyclists, although some of the gradients force the latter to join the former. At the tiny settlement of Grotaig the route takes to a small lane and heads across the hillside away from Loch Ness before dropping down into Drumnadrochit. You actually emerge at Lewiston, which together with nearby Milton were both planned villages built in the 19th century in an attempt to halt rural depopulation. Nearby is a campsite, and a little further on at Strone Point is Urquhart Castle, a ruined 16th century fortification that is amongst the most photographed in Scotland.

Loch Lomond might have a greater surface area but Loch Ness is by far the largest body of freshwater in Britain - its 263,000 million cubic feet of water is more than the all the lakes and reservoirs of England and Wales put together, and deep enough to immerse the Empire State Building! It's said that the water never freezes. No wonder that the legend of a deep-water monster has grown up, and at Drumnadrochit (it means 'ridge of the bridge') there are various exhibitions for the suitably bored or interested. There's such a commercial industry surrounding the monster that you may be forgiven for supposing that it was all invented by the local tourism chief, and although most supposed sightings of Nessie date from the last 70 years there is a record from the 6th century when St Columba is said to have encountered a creature at the northern end of the loch.

 DRUMNADROCHIT ▶ **INVERNESS/BEAULY**, 19/14 miles, 30/22km

Beyond Drumnadrochit there are two choices for the End to Ender. Either you can continue along the Great Glen Way to Inverness (around 17-20 miles or 27-32km) then head 'back' to Dingwall and Alness across the Black Isle;

or you can effectively cut off the corner by heading northwards via Beauly and Strathpeffer. Distance-wise there's actually only a few miles in it, and much will depend on whether you want to visit Inverness or not, or how eager you are to finish the Walk, since there's little more than 140 miles/225km left to John o'Groats.

The Great Glen Way will probably follow a new route over the hillside of Creag Nay, above Drumnadrochit, but at the moment it is still in the process of being finalised. A little further along is Abriachan, a small settlement that made headlines a few years ago when the community became the first to buy their own forest from Forest Enterprise. Beyond Loch Laide the Cycle Route (which has followed the A833 up Glen Convinth to the west before climbing back up to Cragganvallie) and possibly the walking trail join a minor road north eastwards via Blackfold and descend the forested hillside for the approach to Inverness. The capital of the Highlands is, as you would expect, a large and bustling town that boasts all the amenities you could possibly want, including a modern youth hostel. The riverside walk is particularly attractive, and the bouncing Greig Street suspension footbridge across the River Ness is quite an experience!

From Loch Laide and Abriachan, high on the hillside above Loch Ness, the alternative route to Beauly follows some of the Cycle Route in reverse by heading northwards all the way down the lane to the valley floor. A great, new panorama of mountains is revealed at the top, then at the bottom the route continues on quiet back roads via Kiltarlity and Kilmorack to reach Beauly (there's a campsite by Lovat Bridge). The name of this neat and attractive town at the head of the Beauly Firth probably derives from its 13th century Priory, although there's a tale that Mary, Queen of Scots visited the village in 1564 and liked it so much she described it as "beau lieu" (beautiful place).

Inverness TIC: tel 01463 234353. Inverness YH: tel 01463 231771

EDINBURGH ► INVERNESS,
via the Cairngorms approx 175 miles/280km

Compared to the main End to End route via the West Highland Way and Great
Glen Way this far more direct passage from Edinburgh to Inverness via the
Cairngorms will save you 50 miles/80km or more. Since there's no waymarked
trails it offers plenty of room for adjustment - maybe you want to devise your
own route through the Ochil Hills and not stray into Fife at all? And perhaps
you want to take a more easterly route through the Cairngorms via Braemar,
for instance, or miss out the higher ground altogether for a gentler route
via Kingussie?

For Edinburgh city centre to the Forth Bridge see the beginning of this chapter;
then on the far bank the route joins the new Fife Coastal Path for a short
distance to Aberdour or Dalgety Bay before heading north via Kelty, Benarty Hill
and Loch Leven. There are a few local paths and tracks, but inevitably a reliance
too on minor roads and lanes. This combination leads from Kinross via Glenfarg
Reservoir and Forteviot to Perth, the ancient capital of Scotland and the so-
called Gateway to the Highlands. From here it's hillcountry most of the way to
Inverness, first along the banks of the Tay to Luncarty, then north-west along
Glen Shee to reach Aberfeldy (or via the more remoter Glen Almond).
A riverside path leads to Strathtay, a wooded hillside track to Pitlochry, then a
quiet lane and footbridge over the River Garry takes you into Blair Atholl.

At Blair Atholl the End to End Alternative Route hitches up its socks and heads
north-west along Glen Tilt into the heart of the Cairngorm Mountains. Ahead
lies 30 miles/48km of peaceful and unspoilt mountain scenery (and either
camping or a bed at Inverey YH), with the highlight probably the grand Lairig
Ghru crossing under the mighty peaks of Braeriach, Cairn Toul and Ben Macdui
(the fourth, third and second highest mountains in the UK respectively).
Although the terrain can be rough in places there are clear tracks all the way,
and in good weather it's a superb walk with opportunities for Munro-bagging.
However, you must always make sure you're properly equipped, and in adverse
conditions you must take suitable precautions or reassess your route. Other
options include a western route via Glen Feshie to Feshiebridge, or the Lairig
Laoigh crossing further east.

On the northern side of the Cairngorms is the popular outdoor resort of
Aviemore, and from here to Inverness the route is first along a forest track from
the western end of Loch Morlich to Boat of Garten; one of General Wade's now
little-used military roads as far as the summit of Slochd Moor; then deserted
lanes via Findhorn Bridge, Garbole and Starthnairn.

the **FAR NORTH**

INVERNESS TO JOHN O'GROATS
127 miles/204km

INVERNESS/BEAULY TO BRORA
62.5 miles/100km
BRORA TO JOHN O'GROATS
64.5 miles/104km

As John o'Groats draws nearer the pull of the finishing line becomes ever stronger, and the desire for a quick and direct route along the far north-east coast of Scotland is understandable. Beyond Inverness there's plenty of lanes, tracks, and coastal paths that will help you sail past the firths of Beauly, Cromarty and Dornoch. The mountains, although in sight, have retreated for a bit, and the low coastal plain allows good progress northwards, even though there is nothing in the way of recognised walking trails. Some excursions into the hills are possible, and there is access on foot to a number of forests. However, as the towns and villages fall away the coastal belt gets narrower and the land starts to rise, and the final lap of the End to End journey presents one, last problem: the A9.

For other End to Enders on two or four wheels the A9 is not as big a deal, apart from the inclines, but for the pedestrian this fast highway is not an ideal walking route. Until almost Helmsdale you can avoid it by taking to shoreline tracks or minor roads, but north of here the coastal strip between the rough and pathless moorland that plunges down from the mountains narrows to such a tiny clifftop zone that apart from the main road there is virtually nowhere else to walk. There are a few snatches of clifftop, the odd farm track, but by and large if you want to get to John o'Groats as soon as possible the A9 will have to be your route for at least some of the final miles. Just beyond Lybster, however, there's a pleasant and direct open road that heads north across the wide open landscape of Caithness and via the village of Watten to make the concluding day and a half a much more quieter, safer and pleasant affair. One of the few benefits of walking along some of the A9, apart from the road's directness, is that at least the regular distance signs allow you to count down the miles to John o'Groats!

The alternative way to reach John o'Groats is longer, but far more pleasurable, and is outlined at the end of the chapter. From just before Helmsdale you can leave the coastal road for an inland journey up the Strath of Kildonan and across the amazing Flow Country: bogs, lochs, marshes and mountainous wilderness. The route is also along a road, but this time an open, unfenced and comparatively quiet thoroughfare that plunges right across the wild north east corner of Scotland. The final few miles are eastwards, along Scotland's north coast, via Thurso. A further possibility, just an idea here, is to head inland via Bonar Bridge to Lairg, then hill tracks via Loch Choire and Loch Rimsdale to Kinbrace; or north along Strathnaver to the coast at Bettyhill.

What is also obvious from the above is that there are no more long distance trails ahead of you, and as the countryside gets wilder the paths really do get fewer. The End to End route does enjoy some attractive snatches of coastal path, and there is some scope for further off-road

walking along the Alternative Route through the Flow Country; but
for the most part the far north east of Scotland is incredibly bare.
For this reason the final week's walking to John o'Groats is likely to rely
quite heavily on minor roads and lanes. And what will you be feeling,
or thinking, during this final week? You'll have linked the opposite points
of Great Britain, walked your way from one end to the other through a
whole country - or two (or maybe even three) if you prefer. So how will
you celebrate, or mark the achievement? Or perhaps you'll already be
planning for the next big adventure?

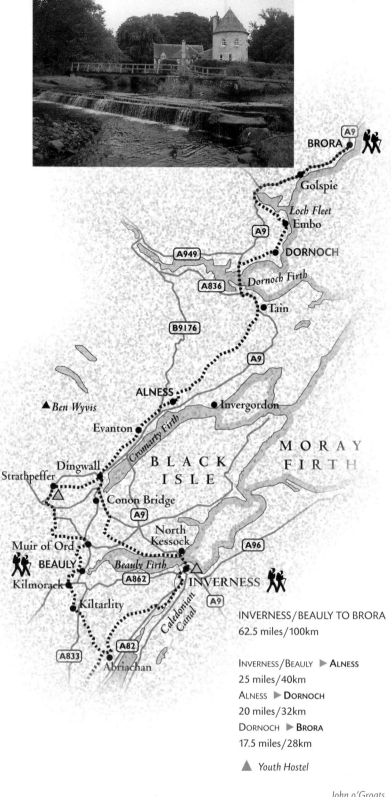

BRORA **A9**

Golspie

Loch Fleet
A9   Embo

A949   DORNOCH

A836   *Dornoch Firth*

B9176   Tain

A9

ALNESS   Invergordon

▲ *Ben Wyvis*

Evanton

Strathpeffer   Dingwall   *Cromarty Firth*

BLACK
ISLE

MORAY
FIRTH

Conon Bridge
A9

North
Kessock   **A96**

Muir of Ord

BEAULY   *Beauly Firth*   **A862**   INVERNESS   **A9**

Kilmorack

Kiltarlity   *Caledonian Canal*

A833   **A82**   Abriachan

INVERNESS / BEAULY TO BRORA
62.5 miles / 100km

INVERNESS / BEAULY ▶ ALNESS
25 miles / 40km
ALNESS ▶ DORNOCH
20 miles / 32km
DORNOCH ▶ BRORA
17.5 miles / 28km

▲ *Youth Hostel*

John o'Groats

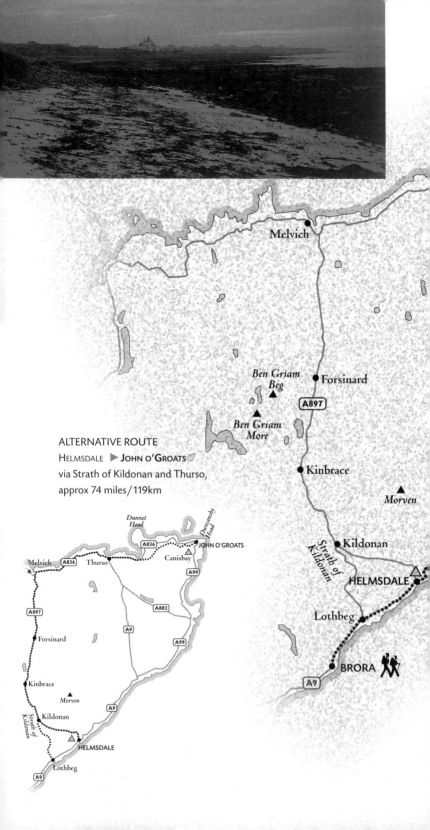

ALTERNATIVE ROUTE
HELMSDALE ▶ **JOHN O'GROATS**
via Strath of Kildonan and Thurso,
approx 74 miles/119km

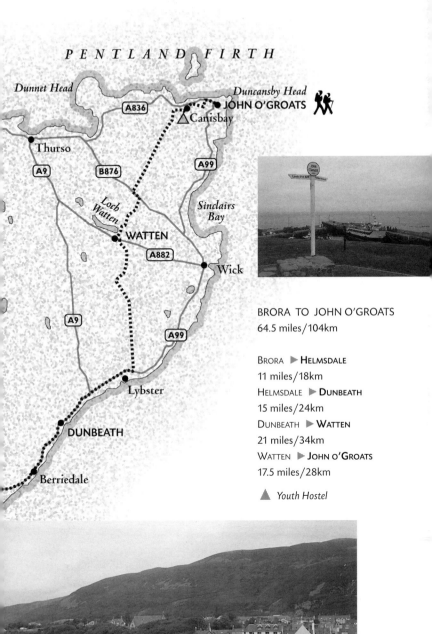

PENTLAND FIRTH

Dunnet Head

Duncansby Head

JOHN O'GROATS

A836

△ Canisbay

Thurso

A9

B876

A99

Loch Watten

Sinclairs Bay

WATTEN

A882

Wick

A9

A99

Lybster

DUNBEATH

Berriedale

BRORA TO JOHN O'GROATS
64.5 miles/104km

BRORA ► **HELMSDALE**
11 miles/18km
HELMSDALE ► **DUNBEATH**
15 miles/24km
DUNBEATH ► **WATTEN**
21 miles/34km
WATTEN ► **JOHN O'GROATS**
17.5 miles/28km

▲ *Youth Hostel*

INVERNESS ▶ **ALNESS**, 25 miles/40km

The busy Kessock Bridge (A9) takes you out of Inverness and across the mouth of the Beauly Firth, then at North Kessock leave the highway for the sanctuary of a peaceful firthside lane westwards. Seals, porpoises and dolphins are all visitors to these waters; while on the other side of the bridge in the Moray Firth Killer whales and minke are occasionally spotted. Further lanes and tracks link Milton with Drynie Park and Biship Kinkell, and then the main road to Conon Bridge and Dingwall. The latter has a history dating back to Viking times, and its name derives from 'Thingvolls' meaning parliament or place of justice. Today it is the county town of Ross-shire. The remaining 9 miles/14km to Alness via Evanton, where there is a campsite, is along direct and mostly quiet back roads that run parallel with the A9. Alness grew up with the oil boom of the 1970s and has plenty of facilities on offer, but like Beauly before it there is a local pride manifested not least in the colourful floral displays and its repeated 'Britain in Bloom' awards. On a hilltop high above Evanton and Alness is the curious Fyrish Monument, a replica of the gateway to Negapatam, an Indian town sacked by General Sir Hector Munro of Novar in 1871, and which was built chiefly to provide work for local people.

Despite the hilly backdrop the coastal plain containing Evanton and Alness is quite flat, which allows good views over the Cromarty Firth, and one of the most peculiar sights is that of massive oil rigs sitting quietly and rather forlornly on their own in the Firth. I understand they are routinely towed into these sheltered waters for repairs, or are simply waiting patiently to be shepherded out to their sites in the North Sea. Nearby Invergordon is the main deep-water port in the Highlands, and was once a major naval base.

For those that have left Loch Ness at Drumnadrochit and have taken the short cut to Beauly the distance to Alness is in fact under 20 miles/32km, but since half of this is along the A862 I suggest a much more pleasant although somewhat circuitous route via Strathpeffer. If the stage seems too much then break the day at Strathpeffer (10 miles/16km), an interesting former Victorian spa resort and home to another SYHA hostel. The leafy settlement was once nationally famous for its spa waters, and these can still be sampled. To reach it follow a combination of lanes and linking tracks via Clashandorran, Aultgowrie Bridge and Marybank - the route will be obvious from the map. The best way to leave Strathpeffer is via Forestry Commission trails over Cnoc Mor and then on to Knock Farrill, a low but distinctive rocky ridge home to rabbits, buzzards and another fascinating vitrified fort. Descend its southern side for a farm lane that runs eastwards into Dingwall; then see above.

Strathpeffer TIC: tel 01997 421415
Strathpeffer YH: tel 01997 421532

Alness ▶ Dornoch, 20 miles/32km

A mostly level stage along straightforward lanes, with an interesting final section across the Dornoch Firth. The town of Tain would be a convenient place to shorten the day, but Dornoch itself is worth more than a casual visit.

From Alness it's a case of heading for the empty lanes at the back of the town which head directly north-eastwards into the forested hills around Scotsburn and out to Tain on the Dornoch Firth. On the OS map the woods go by several names, including Scotsburn Wood and Morangie Forest, but a Forestry Commission leaflet refers to it as Ardross Forest, and it contains several waymarked walking and cycling routes at Aldieburn and elsewhere. It's also worth pointing out that there's no shops or services until you reach Tain, so make sure you visit the baker's at Alness before you set off.

The Ancient and Royal Burgh of Tain traces its roots back to the 11th century, a story well told in the 'Tain Through Time' exhibition on Tower Street. The medieval-looking Tolbooth, and some well-preserved ecclesiastical remains known as the Collegiate Church, are perhaps the most interesting features in the town. As you head for the bridge over the Dornoch Firth you pass the Glenmorangie Distillery, which is open to visitors. Its hard and mineral-rich water comes from the nearby Tarlogie Springs, and the site contains the tallest stills in Scotland (which were originally gin stills bought second-hand from a London gin distiller in 1843). The distillery looks out on to the Dornoch Firth, the northernmost firth on the east coast of Scotland, and whose mudflats are home to large numbers of birds and occasionally seals. Next to the new road bridge there is a sign for John o'Groats (85 miles/137km it reckons), and on the far side of the firth you leave Easter Ross and enter Sutherland. Turn off for the Cuthill lane that leads into Dornoch.

For its relatively small size Dornoch is a fascinating and certainly a handsome place, having grown up around a 13th century cathedral founded by the Bishop of Caithness who moved here from Halkirk. Nearby is the Bishop's Palace, now the Dornoch Castle Hotel; plus the town had a jail and a courthouse. Dornoch was also the site of the last witch-burning in Scotland, when in 1722 a woman called Janet Horne purportedly turned her daughter into a pony. A stone, in the last garden of Carnaig Street, now marks the spot. Many of today's visitors to Dornoch come to play the famous links golf course, established in 1914 and apparently listed number 15 in the world's 100 best courses; or in Madonna's case simply to get married.

Dornoch TIC: tel 01862 810400

Dornoch ▶ Brora, 17.5 miles/28km

You can admire the golf links for yourself as you walk north along the coastal path from Dornoch to Embo; then continue on via Coul to join the lane past the ruined remains of Skelbo Castle on the southern shore of Loch Fleet. This National Nature Reserve was once an open sea loch, but shingle build-up at the mouth has turned it into more of a lagoon that has become vital for all kinds of wildlife. Loch Fleet supports up to 2,000 oystercatchers, plus wigeon and eider ducks. Wintering bar-tailed godwits and Icelandic greylag geese also visit the site, and in summer it is home to common, arctic and little terns. The A9 takes you across the saltmarsh and mudflats and on to Golspie, although a quieter if longer approach is to cut through to the long, sandy beach by Golspie Links.

Golspie was a planned, 19th century village, and although subsequently it wouldn't appear to have grown much more in size it's now the administrative centre for Sutherland. From the northern end there is a pleasant, signposted path along the coastal sward for five miles to Brora. It passes seawards of Dunrobin Castle, the ancestral home of the Earls of Sutherland.

With 189 rooms and parts of the building dating from the early 1300s, Dunrobin claims to be one of Britain's oldest continuously inhabited houses. However, in 1841 the 2nd Duke of Sutherland commissioned Sir Charles Barry (architect of the House of Parliament) and William Leslie to remodel the whole building in a fairy tale style, and the resultant turrets and towers make it look like something out of a Disney movie.

Beyond the castle the path passes an ancient broch known as Carn Liath. These defensive homesteads, built mostly in the late Iron Age, are peculiar to northern Scotland and are commonly associated with the Picts. Essentially brochs are circular stone towers, robust and windowless, but containing a number of rooms, passageways and even a fireplace, and they are often considered the forerunners to the later castles and tower-houses. Carn Liath is believed to be around 2,000 years old, and although only the 12 ft-high walls and entrance doorway are left (it was probably also used by later settlers) you can get a feel for its defensive as well as domestic purpose. A little further on there is more up to date accommodation at Brora, which boasts a lovely beach, plus the nearby Clynelish Distillery.

BRORA ▶ HELMSDALE, 11 miles/18km

The sandy beach north of Brora can be walked for nearly two miles at low tide, otherwise follow the edge of the links past the campsite. As the beach gives way to rocky shelves you eventually have to use one of the railway crossings and join the A9. If you're continuing on the main End to End route up the east coast then simply follow the road as it makes its way along the narrowing coastal strip. Already the high, rough moorland is closing in, and with only a few scattered buildings in sight there is a feeling of constriction and growing remoteness. It may not have the dramatic bays and towering peaks of the North West of Scotland but the further along this east coast you travel the feeling of wildness and emptiness grows.

At a lay-by on the left there is a memorial to the last wolf killed in Sutherland, in 1700; and just beyond is a small turning on the left. If you are heading up the Strath of Kildonan on the Alternative Route across the Flow Country turn off here; otherwise continue on along the road to reach Helmsdale.

The modern development of Helmsdale, like so many of these isolated communities on this coast, was based on the herring fishing industry, the so-called 'silver darlings', and for a while it enjoyed some prosperity. But although the fishing fleets have disappeared the town still has quite a lot going for it, not least its modern visitor centre which boasts an art gallery, cafe and even a herb garden. The exhibition charts the history of the area from the Picts and the Vikings through to the infamous Highland Clearances, plus a 19th century gold rush in the nearby Strath of Kildonan. Below it runs the River Helmsdale, important for salmon fishing, while above are the graceful spans of Telford's bridge (contrast this with the functional but ugly modern equivalent a little downstream). On the far bank is a clock tower monument to the dead of the two World Wars, and below is a preserved ice house, dated 1824, bored into the hillside.

Helmsdale TIC: tel 01431 821640. Helmsdale YH: tel 01431 821577

 HELMSDALE ▶ DUNBEATH, 15 miles/24km

Beyond Helmsdale you enter Caithness, and the walking gets harder. Immediately the ground rises quite dramatically, and the road snakes its way up the steep hillside on to the Ord of Caithness. The high cliffs are punctured by occasional narrow inlets known as 'geos', so take a moment to get your breath back and divert off right to visit the lost village of Badbea. This collection of ruined buildings sits isolated on the open clifftop, commemorated by a tall monument made up of stones from one of the original cottages. About

80 crofters evicted during the Highland Clearances struggled to make a living on this bleak and desperate location in the mid 19th century, and it was said that animals and young children were sometimes tethered to stop them blowing off the cliffs altogether. Despite their perseverance the families ended up emigrating, many to try and start new lives in New Zealand.

The road presses on along the cliffs, and at a couple of points (such as Badbea) there is access to the edge. Thousands of seabirds, including kittiwake, guillemot, fulmar and razorbill, nest on these cliffs in the summer, and if you have binoculars and a head for heights it is quite a spectacle. After plunging down to the hamlet of Berriedale the A9 zigzags up once more. If the wind is blowing hard there is scant protection from the elements, and there are few amenities of any kind. Apparently the average annual windspeed for Caithness is twice that of London. Finally, as you approach Dunbeath, take the lane on the right in order to visit the Heritage Centre. This is situated in the former school where the respected local writer Neil Gunn began his education, and the exhibition includes many artefacts and archives of his work. The themes in Gunn's novels are centred on life in this remote part of northern Scotland, and the power of the landscape as well as the struggle for survival among the poor crofting families. There's a statue of the author, who died in 1973, on the harbourside at Dunbeath.

 DUNEBEATH ▶ WATTEN, 21 miles/34km

The coast road continues northwards via Latheron, where the old parish church now houses the Clan Gunn Museum. Here the history of the clan is detailed from its Norse origins to the present; plus there is evidence which claims to show that it was a Scotsman and not Columbus who discovered America 600 years ago.

The settlement of Lybster was devised and built by Sir John Sinclair in 1849, and it's amazing to think that back in the 19th century its neat little harbour housed the third most important herring fleet in Scotland. Looking inland, from the bridge above Reisgill Burn, the narrow coastal gorge contains one of the very few native broadleaf woodlands in Caithness, otherwise a region largely devoid of any woodland bar a few modern commercial plantations. Birch, hazel, rowan, aspen and willow all grow here in the tight little space.

Just beyond Lybster the coast - and finally the main road - is left behind as you turn inland for the long, direct and usually deserted lane to Watten. The landscape, although not exactly flat, is much less hilly, giving rise to the description of Caithness as the 'Lowlands beyond the Highlands'.

The road heads almost due north as if it, too, is rushing towards John o'Groats as fast as possible. Around you are some scattered dwellings, a few large pockets of conifers, and a lot of wild and open moorland. The only feature of note along the way are the Grey Cairns of Camster, which are well worth examining. These are two large, Neolithic chambered cairns, one round and the other long. They are both pretty much intact, some restoration work having been carried out, and crawling into the low, narrow passages is an odd experience. The cairns were built in the Stone Age, probably around 4,500-5,000 years ago, and more than likely as huge burial tombs for local chieftains and tribal elders.

The open road continues its progress northwards to the small village of Watten, where there is some B&B and a campsite near Loch Watten. However, if you want or need to visit the town of Wick ignore the Watten turning back on the coast and continue along what is now the A99 for a few more miles, and at Sarclet you can pick up a clifftop path for the final approach via the Castle of Old Wick. Distances for this and the last day from Wick to John o'Groats via Sinclairs Bay or the A99 are a couple of miles less than the main route.

Wick TIC: tel 01955 602596

 WATTEN ▶ JOHN O'GROATS, 17.5 miles/28km

There isn't much to say about the final stage of the End to End odyssey in terms of routefinding. Simply thread your way along the uncomplicated minor roads via Lyth, Slickly, Upper Gills and the youth hostel at Canisbay in the general direction of John o'Groats. The pathless tip of Caithness offers few options, except perhaps a stroll along the rough, low clifftop once you hit the shore.

John o'Groats was named after Dutchman Jan de Groot, one of three brothers who arrived in 1496 at the request of King James IV to run the ferry from the mainland to the Orkneys. The charge for the journey was a groat. Prior to this the islands had been part of the combined kingdom of Denmark and Norway, and James was concerned that the Orkneys and in particular the trading benefits associated with them should remain firmly under his control. In fact a passenger ferry still operates during the summer from the tiny harbour below the turrets of the John o'Groats House Hotel (a larger vehicle ferry to Stromness on Orkney runs from Scrabster, near Thurso). Visually the settlement above the harbour is a bit of a mess. There are a few souvenir shops, a post office, a clifftop campsite and the hotel, but they're all scattered about in no particular order, and there's nothing like the organised theme park you encountered at Land's End - which in itself is probably a good thing. The First & Last House is there, as is the famous signpost, and during the summer the tourist coaches and cars roll in and out as you would expect. But there aren't as many as in Cornwall and they don't tend to stay as long.

Make sure you record your arrival at the hotel, then turn your back on
the tourists for the final two miles to Duncansby Head, first along the shoreline
and then the rising clifftop. An easier walk back is along the surfaced lane.
Although Dunnet Head, a few miles further west, is actually the most northerly
point on the British mainland, Duncansby Head is the extreme tip.

It *feels* like the very end. On a clear day there are good views of the Orkney
Islands, and the shipping negotiating the choppy waters of the Pentland Firth.
To the south of the headland, with its gleaming white lighthouse, are the
famous Stacks of Duncansby, rising like huge sharks' teeth from the waves, and
all along these soaring, rugged cliffs are hundreds of screaming seabirds.

John o'Groats TIC: tel 01955 611373
John o'Groats YH: tel 01955 611424
Thurso TIC: tel 01847 892371

So what's it like to finish? The register in the hotel gives an idea of the physical
and mental condition of some of the successful End to Enders striding
or limping into John o'Groats, although a fair majority of them appear to be
cyclists who have taken two or three weeks in the saddle and not ten or eleven
on foot. There's a general feeling of relief at having reached the finishing line,
and having completed an epic journey. Most End to Enders tend to experience
the true satisfaction or elation later on, reflecting on all those memorable
moments (the highs and the lows) over the last few months.
For now you've made it, and that's enough. True, over the years there have
been far longer and more difficult walks than yours, but nevertheless you can
rest assured that the vast majority of people have never and will never take
a walk of 1,150 miles/1,850km in their lives. It is, without doubt,
a special achievement.

Helmsdale ▶ John o'Groats
via Strath of Kildonan and Thurso approx 74 miles/119km

Although longer than the north east coastal route by approximately
21 miles/34km, this alternative ending is somewhat quieter and just as
attractive, but for the first two days across the middle of the Flow Country there
is little in the way of accommodation or other services. For instance, if you
turn off the A9 at Lothbeg for a lovely, tiny lane across the hills to Kildonan you
miss out all the services at Helmsdale (youth hostel, shops, etc). So this stage
is measured further on, from Helmsdale itself, at which point you head inland
(like the railway); and a sign by the A897 gives Melvich, on the north coast,
40 miles/64km or two long days walk away.

The route along the Strath of Kildonan is scenic and full of interest, from
the numerous ruined brochs, cairns and souterrains (underground passages or
chambers) to the tumbling river and the pockets of sheltered woodland.
The Strath was the unlikely site of a Gold Rush in 1868-70 when 500
prospectors flocked to the River Helmsdale in anticipation of making their
fortune. A small shanty settlement appeared called Baille an Or
('the town of the gold'), but inevitably little gold was actually found and the
Duke of Sutherland, who issued expensive licences for tiny plots of land,
made more money than anyone before banning further prospecting when it
began to interfere with his salmon fishing and stalking interests.
Occasional gold panning does still take place near Kildonan.

At Kinbrace the landscape widens out and the lonely, unfenced road
continues through the heart of the Flow Country. 'Flow' is a northern term
used to describe any flat or deep wet peat bog; and over 50% of Caithness and
Sutherland is covered by blanket bog, making it the largest expanse anywhere
in Europe. It's a desolate but evocative place, ringed by several huge peaks,
foremost of which are Ben Griam Mor and Ben Griam Beg. At Forsinard there's
a hotel - geared for well-off salmon fishermen rather than walkers - but the
isolated station building has been turned into the Flow Country Visitor Centre,
with a display by the RSPB who own the nearby nature reserve.

Fourteen miles on is Melvich, on the north coast, with B&B and camping,
then it's time to turn eastwards and follow the coast road towards
John o'Groats. There are a few items of note, including the Dounreay nuclear
power station and the shops and services of Thurso, the most northerly town on
the British mainland. From here it's just 20 miles/32km to John o'Groats,
and from Castletown you can follow quiet back lanes for most of the distance.
Another, final option that will cut out some of the tarmac walking is to leave
the A897 at Forsinain, north of Forsinard, for a cross-country track eastwards
via Altnabreac and Loch More to Westerdale; and from there the road
via Mybster to Watten, or north to Thurso.

INFORMATION

MAPS & GUIDEBOOKS
FURTHER READING
USEFUL ADDRESSES

Maps and guidebooks are listed in route sequence (walking south-north)

Key for Maps
Exp: *Ordnance Survey Explorer*
OL: *Ordnance Survey Outdoor Leisure*
★ End to End route (ie individual trail such as the Camel Trail, Limestone Link or Cotswold Way) shown in part or full on OS map

the SOUTH WEST
LAND'S END TO BATH

LAND'S END ▶ ST BREWARD

Maps:
Exp 102: *Land's End, Penzance and St Ives*
Exp 103: *The Lizard, Falmouth and Helston*
Exp 104: *Redruth & St Agnes*
Exp 105: *Falmouth & Mevagissey*
Exp 106: *Newquay & Padstow*
Exp 109: *Bodmin Moor*

Guidebooks:
National Trail Guide: South West Coast Path (Padstow to Falmouth)
by John Macadam (Aurum Press).
The South West Coast Path (annual information and accommodation guide)
by the South West Coast Path Association.
The Celtic Way
by Val Saunders Evans (Sigma Leisure).
The Land's End Trail
contact Robert Preston, The Chantry, Wilkes Walk, Truro, Cornwall TR1 2UF.

ST BREWARD ▶ TIVERTON

Maps:
Exp 109: *Bodmin Moor*
Exp 112: *Launceston & Holsworthy*
OL 28: *Dartmoor*
Exp 113: *Okehampton*
Exp 114: *Exeter & the Exe Valley*★

Guidebooks:
Two Castles Trail
(leaflet pack from Launceston TIC).
Exe Valley Way
(Devon County Council).

TIVERTON ▶ BATH

Maps:
Exp 114: *Exeter & the Exe Valley*★
Exp 128: *Taunton & Blackdown Hills*
Exp 140: *Quantock Hills & Bridgwater*
Exp 141: *Cheddar Gorge & Mendip Hills West*
Exp 142: *Shepton Mallet & Mendip Hills East*★
Exp 155: *Bristol & Bath*★

Guidebooks:
In Search of the Grand Western Canal *(leaflet pack from Taunton TIC).*
The Limestone Link by Yatton Ramblers *(Ramblers' Association).*

the SEVERN & MIDLANDS
BATH TO EDALE

BATH ▶ TEWKESBURY

Maps:
Exp 155: *Bristol & Bath*★
Exp 167: *Thornbury, Dursley & Yate*★
Exp 168: *Stroud, Tetbury & Malmesbury*★
Exp 179: *Gloucester, Cheltenham & Stroud*★
OL 45: *The Cotswolds*★
Exp 190: *Malvern Hills & Bredon Hill, Tewkesbury*★

Guidebooks:
The Cotswold Way
by Anthony Burton (Aurum Press).
The Cotswold Way Handbook (annual accommodation guide) *by Gloucestershire Area Ramblers' Association.*
The Gloucestershire Way
by Gerry Stewart (Countryside Matters).

TEWKESBURY ▶ PENKRIDGE

Maps:
Exp 190: *Malvern Hills & Bredon Hill, Tewkesbury*★
Exp 204: *Worcester & Droitwich Spa*★
Exp 218: *Kidderminster & Wyre Forest*★
Exp 242: *Telford, Ironbridge & The Wrekin*★
Exp 244: *Cannock Chase & Chasewater*★

Guidebooks:
The Severn Way
(Severn Way Partnership).
The Staffordshire Way
(Staffs County Council).
Where to stay along the Staffordshire Way *(free leaflet by and from Staffs Area Ramblers' Association).*

PENKRIDGE ▶ EDALE

Maps:
Exp 244: *Cannock Chase & Chasewater**
Exp 259: *Derby, Uttoxeter, Asbourne and Cheadle**
OL 24: *Peak District (White Peak)**
OL 1: *Peak District (Dark Peak)**

Guidebooks:
The Staffordshire Way
(Staffs County Council).
Walking the Limestone Way
by Haydock & Allen (Scarthin Books).

the NORTH COUNTRY & BORDERS
EDALE TO EDINBURGH

EDALE ▶ MALHAM

Maps:
OL 1: *Peak District (Dark Peak)**
OL 21: *South Pennines**
OL 2: *Yorkshire Dales (S&W)**

Guidebooks:
National Trail Guide: Pennine Way
(South) *by Tony Hopkins (Aurum Press).*
Pennine Way Accommodation
& Camping Guide (annual guide)
by the Pennine Way Association.
YHA Pennine Way Booking Bureau
see Useful Addresses.

MALHAM ▶ DUFTON

Maps:
OL 2: *Yorkshire Dales (S&W)**
OL 30: *Yorkshire Dales (N&C)**
OL 31: *North Pennines (Teesdale & Weardale)**
OL 19: *Howgill Fells & Upper Eden Valley**

Guidebooks:
National Trail Guide: Pennine Way
(South & North)
by Tony Hopkins (Aurum Press).
Pennine Way Accommodation
& Camping Guide (annual guide)
by the Pennine Way Association.

DUFTON ▶ JEDBURGH

Maps:
OL 19: *Howgill Fells & Upper Eden Valley**
OL 31: *North Pennines (Teesdale & Weardale)**
OL 43: *Hadrian's Wall**
OL 42: *Kielder Water**
OL 16: *The Cheviot Hills**

Guidebooks:
National Trail Guide: Pennine Way
(North) *by Tony Hopkins (Aurum Press).*
Pennine Way Accommodation
& Camping Guide (annual guide)
by the Pennine Way Association.

JEDBURGH ▶ EDINBURGH

Maps:
OL 16: *The Cheviot Hills**
OL 44: *Tweed Valley (Peebles to St Boswells)**
Exp 344: *Pentland Hills, Penicuik & West Linton*
Exp 350: *Edinburgh, Mussellburgh & Queensferry**

Guidebooks:
St Cuthbert's Way
by Roger Smith & Ron Shaw (The Mercat Press), includes route map.
St Cuthbert's Way Accommodation
Leaflet from Jedburgh TIC.
Southern Upland Way
by Roger Smith (The Mercat Press), includes route map.

the HIGHLANDS
EDINBURGH TO INVERNESS

EDINBURGH ▶ ROWARDENNAN

Maps:
Exp 350: *Edinburgh, Mussellburgh & Queensferry**
Exp 349: *Falkirk, Cumbernauld & Livingston*
Exp 342: *Glasgow, Paisely, Rutherglen & Kirkintilloch*
OL 39: *Loch Lomond**

Guidebooks:
Exploring the Edinburgh to Glasgow Canals
by Hamish Brown (The Mercat Press).
The West Highland Way
by Roger Smith (The Mercat Press), includes route map.
West Highland Way Accommodation
Leaflet from WHW Path Manager, Balloch Castle, Balloch G83 8LX (free).

ROWARDENNAN ▶ FORT WILLIAM

Maps:
OL 39: *Loch Lomond**
OL 38: *Ben Nevis & Glen Coe**

Guidebooks:
Exploring the Edinburgh to Glasgow
Canals *by Hamish Brown (The Mercat Press).*
The West Highland Way
by Roger Smith (The Mercat Press),
includes route map.
West Highland Way Accommodation
Leaflet from WHW Path Manager, Balloch
Castle, Balloch G83 8LX (free).

FORT WILLIAM ▶ INVERNESS

Maps:
OL 38: *Ben Nevis & Glen Coe*
Exp 392: *Ben Nevis & Fort William*
Exp 400: *Loch Lochy & Glen Roy*
Exp 416: *Inverness, Loch Ness & Culloden*

the FAR NORTH
INVERNESS TO JOHN O'GROATS

INVERNESS ▶ JOHN O'GROATS

Maps:
Exp 416: *Inverness, Loch Ness & Culloden*
Exp 432: *Black Isle*
Exp 437: *Ben Wyvis & Strathpeffer*
Exp 438: *Durnoch & Tain*
Exp 441: *Lairg, Bonar Bridge & Golspie*
Exp 444: *Helmsdale & Strath of Kildonan*
Exp 450: *Wick & The Flow Country*
Exp 451: *Thurso & John o'Groats*

Maps List/Order Form
For a list and order form for all the maps and
guide books listed contact Cordee Limited,
3a DeMontfort Street, Leicester LE1 7HD,
www cordee.co.uk

Classic End to Ends:
Journey Through Britain
by John Hillaby (Constable).
Hamish's Groats End Walk
by Hamish Brown (Paladin).

Coastline End to Ends:
Turn Right at Land's End
by John Merrill (Oxford Illustrated Press).
And the Road Below
by John Westley (Meridian Books).
Two Feet, Four Paws-the Girl who
Walked her Dog 4,500 miles
by Spud Talbot-Ponsonby
(Summersdale Publishing).
The Sea on Our Left
by Shally Hunt (Summersdale Publishing).

Personal End to Ends:
Britain's Winding Road
by Roy Eardley.
One Man and his Dog go Walkies
by Noel Blackham.
A Walker's Diary
by Robin Moore.
Return Journey
by Fred Noonan.
End to End Stuff
by John Simcock.
One Woman's Walk: from Land's End
to John o'Groats
by Shirley Rippin.
I walked from Land's End
to John o'Groats
by Krister Andersen.
A Grandparents' Guide from Land's
End to John o'Groats
by Eileen and Herbert Witherington.

Practical Considerations:
The Rambler's Yearbook &
Accommodation Guide
(Ramblers' Association).
The Long Distance Walkers' Handbook
(Long Distance Walkers' Association,
A&C Black).
Out in the Country: where you can go
and what you can do
(Countryside Agency).
Rights of Way: A Guide to the Law in
Scotland
(Scottish Rights of Way Society).
Navigation for Walkers
by Julian Tippett (Cordee)

Camping & Caravanning Club
Greenfields House, Westwood Way,
Coventry CV4 8JH.

Countryside Agency Publications
PO Box 125, Wetherby,
West Yorks LS23 7EP,
tel 0870 120 6466.

The End to End Club
Custom House, Land's End, Sennen,
Cornwall TR19 7AA,
tel 01736 871501.

The John o'Groats House Hotel
John o'Groats, Caithness KW1 4YR
tel 01955 611203.

The Land's End Hotel
Land's End, Sennen, Cornwall TR19 7AA,
tel 01736 871844.

Long Distance Walker's Association
Bank House, High Street, Wrotham,
Sevenoaks, Kent TN15 7AE.

Ordnance Survey
Romsey Road, Maybush,
Southampton SO16 4GU,
tel 08456 050505.

Pennine Way Association
29 Springfield Park Avenue, Chelmsford,
Essex CM2 6EL.

Ramblers' Association
2nd floor, Camelford House,
87-90 Albert Embankment,
London SE1 7TW,
tel 020 7339 8500.

Scottish Youth Hostels Association
7 Glebe Crescent, Stirling FK8 2JA,
tel 01786 891400.

Scottish Rights of Way Society
24 Annandale Street, Edinburgh EH7 4AN.

South West Coast Path Association
Windlestraw, Penquit, Ermington,
Devon PL21 0LU.

Youth Hostels Association
Trevelyan House, Dimple Road, Matlock
Derbyshire DE4 3YH
tel 0870 870 8808.

YHA Pennine Way Booking Bureau
YHA Northern Region, PO Box 11,
Matlock, Derbys DE4 2XA,
tel 01629 581061.